Reminiscence:
Life of A
Country Doctor

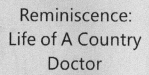

Reminiscence:
Life of A Country
Doctor

Carl Matlock MD

Reminiscence: Life of A Country Doctor

Published in the United States by Matlock Publishing

ISBN: 978-0-9600521-3-4 Paperback

ISBN: 978-0-9600521-4-1 Ebook

Cover and interior design by Carl Matlock

Editing by Christy Distler, Avodah Editorial Services

Cover Images by shutterstock.com

First Edition

DEDICATION

I once again wish to express my sincere thanks to my loving wife, Janet Matlock. She laboriously read my manuscript, making many valuable contributions to the work. She continues to be my first editor.

This book is dedicated to our five grandchildren in order of birth:

Jared Matlock, Cameron Survance, Janae Matlock, Patrick Survance, and Reece Rundell.

These five young people have made our lives complete.

Acknowledgments

I want to especially thank Avodah Editorial Services and Christy Distler in particular for editing my manuscript for this work. She has greatly enhanced my effort to publish *Reminiscence: Life of A Country Doctor*.

CONTENTS

Preface

The people and places in this work are fictional but based on real life experiences from my days of medical practice. The only exceptions are the stories about my family and the Indianapolis hospitals. Those are certainly real.

Many wonderful young ladies worked for me over the years, and the two named in the book represent all of those faithful and dedicated healthcare workers. I owe them much for their service and love of people that so greatly enhanced my medical practice.

The patient encounters do represent real events but are composites of the many patients and experiences I've had in caring for people over the years. There is no intent to in any way represent a living or deceased patient in a derogatory manner. That is why the patient encounters are dramatized and fictionalized.

The treatments detailed in this account are by no means recommended for use by any current readers. They are very much features of the 1970s and do not constitute current recommendations for therapy. I wanted to keep the book as realistic as possible by referring to that which was available during the time frame represented. Dear reader, please consult your physician before embarking on any new therapy or medication.

I graduated from Indiana University School of Medicine in 1971, and we were told that if we didn't keep up with the study of medicine, we would be hopelessly outdated in five years. Thus I spent 47 years practicing and studying medicine. I lived it and loved it. Our professors were so right. I lived to see the development of CT scanners, MRIs, electronic records, and electronic stethoscopes, to name a few. Medical advances during my lifetime have been breathtaking. New medications for diseases once thought to be hopeless are little short of astounding. Treatment of heart disease and stroke disorders are so revolutionary as to be nearly unbelievable. It has been my privilege to witness and experience this dynamic progress.

Yet something seems to have been lost along the way. The personal aspect of medicine has been largely displaced by technology. Physicians are forced to spend more time taking care of computerized medical records than real living, breathing patients. Just like a business, we are now supposed to call our patients *clients*. It all becomes so very impersonal at times.

This book is written to reflect on what has been, what is, and what might be. If one young physician reads this story and leaves his or her computer behind, focusing attention on the patient sitting across the room, waiting to finish the electronic record until right after the visit, I believe that intangible something we call the doctor-patient relationship could be enhanced and achieved.

Carl Matlock, MD

Chapter 1:

Babies and Christmas in September

Startled from sound sleep by a discordant jangling, I turned onto my side and grabbed for the source of irritation, hoping to quickly silence the strident harsh ringing tones threatening to awaken my family, but merely managed to knock the phone receiver to the floor. I jumped from bed in the dark, managing to stub my toe, and searched for the disembodied voice coming from the darkness somewhere below.

As I hopped about on one foot, searching for my slippers and the telephone, Janet, my lovely and longsuffering wife, switched on the small lamp on her bedside table and came to the rescue. One of our six-month-old twins, David or Diane, began fussing in the next room. Janet just smiled, retrieved the receiver from beneath the bed, and went to check on the children. The clock said it was almost 3:00 a.m.

Receiver in hand, I finally answered. "Hello. I'm sorry, I accidentally knocked the phone off the hook and couldn't find it in the dark. Who's calling, please?"

"Dr. Matlock, it's Mildred Long at the hospital. One of your patients, Betty Murray, just checked into labor and delivery. I think you had better start this way as soon as you can. This is her third pregnancy, and she has a history of rapid delivery."

I tried to clear the cobwebs from my sleep-deprived brain. "How far along is she now?"

"She is already dilated to six centimeters with hard contractions about three minutes apart. As I said, you'd better hurry."

"Thanks, Mildred. I'll throw myself together and head that way. See you soon."

With chagrin, I saw that our three-year-old daughter, Cindy, was now awake. The twins had quieted down, but Cindy had moseyed into our room clinging to Janet's hand and clutching her favorite teddy bear in her other arm. Placing her bear on the mattress, she reached up to be helped into bed. I laid her on the bed with her curly head on my pillow, gently tucked her in, and kissed her forehead.

She smiled up at me. "Thank you, Daddy." Then she promptly closed her eyes and snuggled beside her mother, who'd also gotten in bed.

"Sorry, dear. I didn't mean to awaken the entire household."

"It's all right. The twins are resting now, and Cindy asked to come to bed with me. You're having a busy month so far with your OB patients. How many does this make for September?"

"This will be the ninth or tenth, I think. I have to hurry. She's in hard labor according to Mildred Long, and you know Mildred. She rarely miscalculates. She's probably delivered more babies in our hospital than most of the doctors."

Within three or four minutes, I stepped out the front door, closing it softly and locking it behind me. My brown-and-yellow 1972 Ford station wagon awaited me in the driveway, illuminated by the soft glow of the streetlight.

Fifteen minutes later, I arrived at the hospital and ran up the stairway to the third floor where our labor and delivery patients were cared for by an excellent staff of nurses and nursing assistants.

6

Mildred Long glanced my way. "You'd better hurry. She's completely dilated at ten centimeters now. We're taking her into the delivery room."

"Be right there," I called over my shoulder as I dashed into the doctors' dressing room, where I met the anxious spouse.

Betty's husband had just changed into scrubs to attend the delivery. "Thank goodness you're here, Doc. I was really worried. Her labor was much harder than with our others."

"I'm sure everything's okay, William. Mildred Long is an outstanding nurse. She would've warned me if anything seemed amiss. Come on. Let's get in there. You stand by your wife's head, and if you feel faint, sit down on the stool in the corner."

"I'll be okay. You let me watch the last time too, and I really appreciate it. The older doctors would never let the husband in the room."

In the delivery room, I went right to the end of the delivery table. I only had time to put on my gloves. No time for scrubbing or gowning since the baby was head first and crowning at that very moment. I gently received the head to control the delivery and suctioned out the nares with an infant nasal bulb. The remainder of the delivery progressed rapidly, and William Junior entered the world bellowing his displeasure with full-throated screaming and crying, Apgar score of 10/10. He was a seven-pound ten-ounce boy, bald but beautiful, born at 3:35 a.m.

After clamping and cutting the umbilical cord, I placed Will Junior in his mama's arms and felt anew the joy of having assisted a new life into the world. William Senior and Betty exchanged loving glances as they admired the most recent addition to their family. The nursing assistant, Sharon Cunningham, obligingly snapped pictures of the threesome for their family photo album.

The placenta delivered spontaneously within a few minutes, and a dose of Oxytocin was given to assure uterine contraction thereby preventing excessive bleeding. A quick examination revealed no pelvic or vaginal lacerations. Mildred beamed at everyone as she took charge of the infant, making sure he was documented properly with his own little ID bracelet and ink imprints of his feet.

After congratulating the family, I checked my watch. 3:45 a.m. Mildred Long was right as usual. It was good that I had hurried. If only they were all that easy!

Forty-five minutes later, I had dictated the delivery note, examined little Will, signed the birth certificate, and made a last-minute stop to check on the Murrays. Then passing by the nursing station, I nodded to Mildred. "Thanks for your help. You and Sharon did a great job as usual. I'm going home to shave, shower, and get ready for work. It's too early to make rounds now. Most of my patients don't like being awakened at 4:30 a.m., so I'll be back around 7:00. I'll check back with OB day shift afterward. Call if you need me. I forgot my pager in the rush to get here, but it'll only take about thirty minutes to get home."

Mildred beamed with pride. "Thank you, Doctor. It's always my pleasure. I really love what I do as a nurse."

***

I shivered once as I exited our one-hundred-bed hospital in Glen Falls and made my way to the doctors' parking lot. The chilly morning breeze warned of impending seasonal change. In those days, my pager only beeped, warning me to call the hospital operator for a message. Since cell phones didn't exist in the 1970s, a beep meant urgently hunting for a pay telephone if I happened to be away from my home or office.

My next OB patient was not due for another three weeks, so I felt comfortable making a leisurely drive home. I would need to pick up my beeper for the day's work, but I didn't think I needed it at the time.

Avoiding the interstate for a time of relaxation, I chose my favorite drive through the back roads to my home in Glen Oaks. The full moon illuminated my drive past familiar farms and small towns. I mentally checked off the homes of my patients where I made house calls. My family medical practice was very demanding, but I wouldn't have traded places with anyone in the world. I loved practicing in rural Indiana, caring for the gracious people who honored me by calling me their doctor.

At home, my lovely wife prepared a delicious breakfast while I got ready for the rest of the day.

***

Following rounds on my hospital patients later that morning, I took the interstate back to Glen Oaks. I did my best to start seeing patients on time at 9:00 a.m. in the office. My third cup of coffee for the morning helped keep me alert and ready for the day.

I entered the office and greeted Christine, my young receptionist. "Betty Murray had a baby boy this morning. William Junior arrived in a hurry at 3:35. The Murrays are all doing very well."

Clasping her hands together, Christine smiled. "That's great, Doc. Donna will be jealous that I found out before she did. Betty was to have been the first patient this morning, so you'll have a few minutes to rest. I'll bet you're tired."

"You're right about that. I've been hitting the coffee more than usual this morning, but I'm fine. That's one less delivery to worry about, and no one else is due for about three weeks. By the way, is Donna here yet? I thought that was her car outside."

"She's here. We had a walk-in first thing this morning. She's in the back checking him in now. His name is Ronnie Johnson. He's seventy-seven years old and seems a little confused. He called our town marshal, Tom Collins, and reported a disturbance at about 6:00 a.m. You know Tom. He checked on Mr. Johnson and immediately got the next-door neighbor, Lance Jones, involved. Tom's already back at the drug store having his morning coffee and donuts. Not much disturbs his day for long. Lance is back there with Donna and Mr. Johnson now. It seems that Mr. Johnson has no close relatives, so Lance brought him in to see you."

I never ceased to marvel at the extensive information Christine always seemed to have about our town and its residents. "What was the nature of the disturbance Mr. Johnson reported?"

Rolling her eyes and smiling enigmatically, she hesitated. "Well … you'll find out. I don't want to spoil it for you." Christine was a good soul, but she sure enjoyed a flair for the dramatic.

I shrugged and shook my head, then walked on back to the lab, which was spacious enough to also serve as a medication room and break area for the staff to relax and have lunch. The coffee was already made, and I poured my fourth cup, savoring the fresh, delightful aroma of hot black Folgers dark-blend coffee.

I rested in one of our metal kitchen-style chairs, seated at a white metal table for four to six people while I continued to enjoy the morning. A large picture window at the back of the office afforded me a view of our closest neighbor's farm. His horses were peacefully grazing on the last of the summer's short grass. He would be forking them hay before long.

As I finished my coffee, Donna entered the lab shaking her head. "Wow. You have your work cut out with this poor man. He's really confused and has no one to look after him. I'm not sure what you'll do for him. But, before you start, you have to tell me about Betty and the new baby. I'm dying to hear all about it."

For the next several minutes, I related the details of the birth of Will Junior. Christine slipped into the lab too, wanting to hear all about it as well. I was indeed blessed to have caring young ladies working for me; they were a vital part of the practice, making the most nervous and self-conscious patients feel welcome in our office.

The sound of the front door opening and closing alerted us that patients were beginning to arrive. The ladies went back to work, and I made my way to exam room 1, then pulled the chart from the door rack to briefly peruse Donna's notes before entering. After stepping inside, I greeted Lance Jones and turned to introduce myself to Mr. Johnson.

Before I could say a word, he stood up and gripped my right hand. "My friends call me Ronnie. You must be the doc. I sure hope you can figure out what's wrong at my house. Marshal Collins told me you could straighten everything out with those people on the roof. I've never see'd the like in my life. You can't imagine the racket they made stompin' on my ceiling. The old man was friendly, and I've a notion who he is, but I didn't like the smelly animals he had all over my house top."

"Have a seat, Mr. Johnson," I said, "and let's start at the beginning, please."

"Ronnie," he insisted.

"What's that? Oh yes. You prefer that I call you Ronnie."

I helped him back to his chair while he smiled down at me. Ronnie was every bit of six feet five inches tall, even though mildly stooped when standing. His long thin face, wrinkled like highway markings on a crowded map, seemed bewildered but kind in appearance. His complexion was a sallow yellow color, but his eyes were deep blue. Dark brown rivulets from chewing tobacco stains coursed down his chin while sparse long white whiskers formed a ragged goatee, giving him a distinctive appearance.

"You never see'd anything quite like me, did ya, Doc? I can tell the way you're lookin' at me. I bet you'd like to have a set of whiskers just like mine. My old pappy had him a beautiful set of whiskers. He lived to be ninety or so, or at least to eighty. My mammy didn't have no beard, just a kindly smile. Why did ya want to see me? The marshal said ya did."

By this time, he was somewhat winded from talking and moving about to greet me. I noted his vital signs as recorded: pulse 110, respirations 24, BP 180/95, temperature unobtainable due to constant talking. Donna also noted his swollen legs and the stale smell of urine.

"Ronnie, the marshal said you reported some type of trouble this morning."

"He did?" Pausing to stroke his thin goatee, he finally nodded. "Ya know. He did say somethin' about havin' trouble. What do ya reckon the trouble was? Did somebody get hurt? Did someone go to jail?" Smiling at me, he winked. "I bet ya can't guess what I had for breakfast this mornin'."

Taking in the yolk stains and splotches of dried coffee on his shirt, I grinned back. "Let me guess. Eggs and coffee."

He shook his head in amazement, then directed his attention to Lance. "He's smart. Ya know it?"

"Just a moment, Ronnie," I said. "I want to have Donna come back and help you to the bathroom. We need to check a urine specimen. I want to make sure you don't have an infection."

"Sure 'nuff. Whatever you say. You're the doc."

11

While Donna led Ronnie down the hall, I took the opportunity to speak with Lance. "How did you get involved, other than being his neighbor?"

"It's a long story, but he's a nice old man who's always struck me as a little odd. He's a great gardener, in spite of his many eccentricities. He's kept my family supplied with all kinds of vegetables the last two summers. I tried to pay him, but he acted offended. At any rate, I felt that I owed him something in return. My wife and I pick up little cakes and desserts that he likes from the grocery store. He accepts them but refuses any other form of payment. As we got better acquainted with Ronnie, we found that he has no living relatives as far as he knows. It's really sad. So we've tried to be a help to him as much as we can."

"Does he have any resources available to help him now?"

"I'm pretty sure he doesn't. He retired a few years ago on a small pension. I believe he owns his home, but he has little else. He recently asked if I would help balance his bank account. Believe me, it was totally confusing. After hours sitting with him and figuring, I finally balanced his statement. He has less than one hundred dollars in his account. His small pension of three hundred dollars per month plus his Social Security is nearly wiped out each month by his routine bills, and he doesn't even use air conditioning or other conveniences like most people. I promised him that I would do what I could to help, but honestly, I don't know where to start."

"You've already done a lot to help," I assured him. "I want to examine him better when Donna brings him back to the room, but from his appearance, he needs to be hospitalized. Did you notice how breathless he gets when speaking more than a few words?"

"I sure did. That's been getting worse the last two weeks. I just convinced him to come see you this morning. The confusion is something fairly recent."

Soon Donna escorted Ronnie back into the room. "The urine is clear, and the dipstick checked out fine. I have a sample under the microscope in the lab for you to look at when you finish here."

She helped him undress and put on a gown, assisted him onto the exam table, and placed a folded sheet over his legs. As she left the room to go attend to the patients who were arriving, Lance got up to go the waiting room, but Ronnie asked him to stay.

I began my visual inspection while trying to put Ronnie at ease. "Can you tell me any more about what led you to call the marshal this morning?"

"Sure can. Santa Claus and a bunch of reindeer landed on my roof about five this morning. The stompin' and noise on the roof 'bout drove me crazy. When Tom Collins got there, I think he scared 'em off. But they came right back when he left."

"Do you really believe Santa Claus was on your roof this morning?"

"Been thinkin' 'bout that. Doesn't make much sense, does it? It's too early for him to show up."

"Right you are, Ronnie," I said. "Maybe you had a bad dream."

"Could be you're right, Doc."

Since Ronnie seemed comfortable with me, I proceeded to the examination, which revealed a mildly red and swollen tongue, paleness of the conjunctivae (inner eyelids), pale fingernail beds, loss of erythema (redness) to the palmar creases, and general pale complexion throughout. His breathing was mildly labored with prolonged expiratory phase, suggesting possible chronic obstructive pulmonary disease from his admitted previous years of smoking.

I could also hear moist rales at the lung bases posteriorly and a loud S3 gallop rhythm characteristic of congestive heart failure. He had 1+ pitting pedal (foot) edema up to the mid-calves, also consistent with heart failure, and diminished sensation in his feet to vibration as tested with my tuning fork applied to the ankle. A rectal exam disclosed brown stool that was Hematest negative for blood.

"Do your toes tingle?" I asked.

"Come to think of it, they do feel different."

"Is your tongue sore? It looks a little red and swollen."

He nodded. "Sometimes it hurts."

"Have you been eating a balanced diet? You're not a vegetarian, are you?"

"A vege... what? I don't know what that means." Ronnie scratched his head, thinking. "Well, you mightn't call it balanced, but

I sure like eggs and milk. I have a little flock of chickens. Boy, are they good layers."

"If you like eggs, you're likely getting plenty of B12 in your diet. That's good."

Upon checking his urine, I found it to be completely normal. A common cause of confusion in the elderly is urinary tract infection, but I could now rule that out as a contributing factor. Taking some time to clear my thoughts, I poured another cup of coffee and took a couple of sips before returning to the room with a plan I hoped he would accept.

"Ronnie, you're anemic. Low on blood in other words. I also detect what we call congestive heart failure. That means that your lungs have some fluid back-up in them, making you short of breath. Needless to say, you smoked too much when you were a young man, which didn't help at all."

Ronnie winked at me and smiled, nodding his head.

"I think we can make you feel a lot better, but you need X-rays of your lungs, an EKG to check your heart, and blood work to see why you're low on blood. The quickest and best way to do that is in the hospital for a few days. Would you be willing to do that?"

Ronnie glanced at Lance. "Well, I'll do 'er if he thinks it's okay."

"Sure, Ronnie," Lance said. "It's the right thing to do, as Doc says. I'll take you in my car and will visit you every day. Okay?"

Ronnie just smiled and nodded once more.

Relieved by his response, I returned to the lab. There I used our wall phone to call the hospital's nursing supervisor and arranged for his admission, blood work, and other tests. I would see him after my evening meal and review his lab work. In those days, I normally made rounds at least twice a day, sometimes more often depending on admissions and emergencies. But first I had thirty-five more patients to see, a moderate day in the office.

Chapter 2:

Anemia and Acute Delirium

That evening, I made my way to the medical ward on 2 North and retrieved Ronnie Johnson's chart from the circular revolving chart rack, then went to the doctor's cubicle to review the laboratory data, chest X-ray, and EKG.

1. Blood work: Hemoglobin 7.3 and hematocrit 21.5

    with megaloblastic appearance on peripheral smear;

    hypersegmented granulocytes; mild leukopenia and

    thrombocytopenia. (Normal hemoglobin for an adult

    male is 14–16 and normal hematocrit is 42–48 with

    some decrease with normal aging, though laboratories

    vary somewhat on normal values.)

2. Chemistries: Moderately elevated LDH and indirect

    bilirubin. Mildly elevated BUN and creatinine.

    Normal chemistries otherwise.

3.   Chest X-ray: Moderate cardiomegaly with mild CHF

(congestive heart failure) and moderate COPD

(chronic obstructive pulmonary disease).

4.   EKG: Consistent with LVH (left ventricular

hypertrophy). No evidence of MI (myocardial

infarction, commonly known as heart attack).

Mary Adams, the evening charge nurse, stopped outside my cubicle. "How are you tonight? Working late as usual, I see."

"Yes. I'm concerned about Mr. Johnson. How is he doing?"

"He responded well to the dose of Lasix you gave him. His output is about 1500 ml so far and he is breathing better. His pulse has slowed to 95, and he looks and acts more comfortable."

"It looks like he has megaloblastic anemia, probably B12 or folic-acid deficiency."

"Can you explain his labs so I can give a clear report to the night shift at eleven?"

"Sure. His hemoglobin and hematocrit are quite low. I think this developed slowly, because his heart is tolerating it fairly well with only mild CHF. His red blood cells are larger than normal, likely fragile, because he appears to have mild hemolysis ongoing as reflected in the elevated LDH and indirect bilirubin. They're released during breakdown of RBCs. Also, his WBCs are hypersegmented, consistent with megaloblastic anemia, either pernicious anemia or folic-acid deficiency. He isn't a drinker and I really suspect PA (pernicious anemia). His heart failure is probably a result of the load on his cardiovascular system, trying to pump enough blood to perfuse his vital organs."

I glanced at the labs again. "His BUN and creatinine reflect diminished renal function due to age and poor blood flow. Thankfully, his renal function is not critically impaired. I expect it to improve as he recovers. Could you please notify the lab that I want to start a Schilling test in the morning? That will help in the diagnosis and actually begin treatment with B12. Meanwhile, go ahead and start the packed RBCs tonight to help his cerebral and cardiac blood flow. Give the first unit slowly over six hours, and call me if he has any problems with the transfusion."

Mary looked pensive for a moment. "Don't worry about that for one minute. If he has any complications, you'll be the first to know." Then folding her arms, she looked at me over the top of her wire-rimmed glasses. "Now run along home and don't write any more orders for me to take off tonight. Be a good sport, please."

***

Over the next few days in the hospital, Ronnie progressively improved in both mentation and cardiac function. His Schilling test, a measurement of B12 absorption, is rarely done these days. His response to B12 injections and better nutrition did wonders to improve his mental status and general health. The CHF resolved nicely, and digoxin (a nearly obsolete medication for heart failure today) was able to eventually be tapered off his regimen. He continued on a low dose of Hydrodiuril, a mild thiazide diuretic for his hypertension, but only after his renal function improved.

Social services became involved with Ronnie because of his lack of a stable family support system. He remained hospitalized for two weeks as he convalesced. In the 1970s, hospitals had no government or insurance pressure to discharge patients, which was a very good thing in this case.

A couple of days before planned discharge, I walked into Ronnie's room to find him sitting up smiling and holding a coherent conversation with Jane Dobson, our social worker.

"Good morning, Jane," I greeted her. "How is our patient doing today?"

Jane beamed. "He's doing great. We've been discussing what might be best for him on release, and he's interested in going to Friendly Care Manor."

"Great. What made you decide in favor of nursing home care?"

Ronnie grinned and winked wickedly at me. "I haven't had food this good in a long time." After pausing for effect, he continued, "But what really decided me was all these beautiful, nice young ladies takin' such good care of me. I wouldn't get any of that at home."

"What are you going to do with your property and your chickens?" I asked.

"We were just talking 'bout that too. Jane and me, we talked with Lance. He's willin' to be my guardian and POA. He'll help me take care of my animals and property. He's a good man."

I looked at Jane. "What do you think?"

"I've done a thorough investigation of the situation, including a state police background check of Lance Jones and his family, and—"

"That weren't necessary," Ronnie interrupted. "He's a good man."

"Right you are, Ronnie, but it's part of my job," she said. "He and his family have a sterling reputation in the community. He's the ideal person for your POA and guardianship."

Ronnie smiled again. "That's better. I don't like my friend bein' questioned by the police. He ain't done nothin' wrong."

Two days later, Ronnie was discharged to the nursing home as planned.

***

After discharge, Ronnie had a UGI done to evaluate his stomach, but it appeared normal except for mild atrophic gastritis, again consistent with the diagnosis of pernicious anemia, in which intrinsic factor secretion from the gastric mucosa is impaired. (Intrinsic factor is one of the necessary metabolic requirements for absorption of B12.) His tingling of the extremities improved somewhat but never resolved completely, and his blood count and peripheral blood smear eventually reverted to normal. He strongly advised me that he wanted no more UGI studies, as he didn't like the taste of the concoction and he was too old to treat if anything serious was found. He required no further hospitalizations and enjoyed the visits from his adopted people, the Lance Jones family.

Ronnie Johnson spent several years in the local nursing home, comfortable, well nourished, and receiving the medical care he needed. He quickly became a favorite of the nursing staff and had no further problems with anemia or heart failure. Several years later, Ronnie died peacefully in his sleep. He was a good soul and was sorely missed by those who came to know him as I did.

Many times since then, I've had patients vociferously rail against going to a nursing home for rehab or chronic care. I was sometimes told that no one likes it, but then I thought of Ronnie and his contagious smile of satisfaction every time I called on him at Friendly Care Manor. Maybe he was an exception, but the nursing and ancillary staff at the home certainly improved his quality of life as he peacefully and comfortably lived out his days, no longer confused and sick.

Chapter 3:

OB Day

Another all-nighter, as we used to say in med school. Yawning, I shook my head, trying to wake up as I carefully steered my Ford station wagon into the office parking lot behind the building.

As I entered the back door into the spacious combined lab and break area, Christine, the office assistant and receptionist, greeted me. "Good morning, Dr. Matlock. It's a beautiful fall day in Glen Oaks. After last night's frost, the trees will really be turning color. Temperature up to seventy-five today, or so the weatherman says."

"Good morning. How're you today?"

"Fine and raring to go. Smell the fresh Folgers brew that I just finished making? Just what the doctor ordered. All's well with the world."

I did my best to suppress another yawn. "You are so right. Elizabeth Condor had her baby last night. I had about two hours of broken sleep. Bring on the coffee, please."

Christine clapped her hands and whirled in a circle. "I can hardly wait to see the new baby. What did she have?"

The enthusiasm of my staff never ceased to amaze me. "She had boy number four, a squalling eight-pound two-ounce bundle of joy. If he's half as active as the other three, labor and delivery will have seemed like a picnic in the park."

After I recited all the vital statistics, we heard Donna unlocking the front door for business. Christine turned to open the door into the hallway and looked back expectantly over her shoulder.

"Can I be the one to tell Donna?"

"You go right ahead. But first, do we have a big day scheduled? I have to admit to being very tired this morning."

Christine flushed with excitement as she called back, "Not too bad, at least not this morning. It's fairly light because of OB day, you know."

Before I could ask another question, the door slammed shut behind her, and I heard her calling to Donna, "Just wait until you hear the news. Elizabeth Condor had her fourth son this morning. I know Doc was worried about her, and ..."

As their voices faded into the outer office, I collapsed into a chair in the break area with my fourth cup of coffee for the day, or was it the fifth? Slowly relishing sips of hot coffee, I felt a little relief that the day was "not too bad," whatever that meant.

In an attempt to protect expectant mothers from contagious illnesses, Tuesday mornings were dedicated to our OB patients as much as possible. With Donna's assistance, we could easily see fifteen or twenty established patients as well as one or two new ones in that time frame. We also did postpartum exams, including physicals on the new babies, on Tuesdays.

Soon Donna had four rooms filled, vital signs completed, and urine dipstick results hanging in the chart slots outside the doors. Most often, OB day was a happy day in the office as I examined and counseled basically healthy expectant mothers. Donna assisted on diet, weight control and maintenance, and a multitude of health-related issues.

Office hours started at 9:00 a.m., and by noon we had seen twenty patients, including a couple of infants. When the last patient exited the front door, I plopped down in my favorite chair in the break area, sighing with relief. (This was still in the early days, when I took an hour off for lunch. As the practice grew, I learned to eat a sandwich while standing up and reviewing charts in the back room, then I'd see patients all through the noon hour.)

I gave Donna some cash for a hamburger and a Diet Coke, and she and Christine locked the front door as they left for Barry House's drug store on Main Street. His establishment not only boasted a pharmacy and old-fashioned lunch and soda fountain, but also a general farm and country store with an amazing supply of goods for the rural community.

For a few minutes, I enjoyed watching the neighbor's horses grazing in the field behind the office, but it wasn't long before I slumped in the chair and slept. I awakened, moderately refreshed, at the sound of the front door opening as the ladies returned from lunch. Donna brought my favorite from the drug store, a juicy hamburger on a bun with dill pickles, a gourmet's delight to my way of thinking.

She counted out my change before returning to the front office and waiting room. "Take your time. There's no one here yet. We only have twelve scheduled to see this afternoon. Christine is trying to contact the later appointments to see if they can arrive earlier. At least we can try."

These young ladies who worked for me were top notch.

"Thanks to both of you. I appreciate your concern. I really do need to get home and rest for a while. Unless there are emergencies, schedule any call-ins for tomorrow. Hopefully I'll be more rested by then."

***

The afternoon wore on until there was only one patient left to see at 3:30 p.m. I took a brief coffee break—my seventh cup—while Donna prepared the patient for evaluation.

She was frowning when she entered the lab where I sat drinking coffee. "Edward and Kathy Dixon are here with little Taylor. You delivered him about four months ago. I'm not sure what's wrong, but his weight is only in the twenty-fifth percentile for his age, about thirteen-point-five pounds. I checked on his birth weight, and it was nine pounds when you delivered him. He's growing longer, but he sure looks thin."

That didn't sound good. "Anything else?"

"I think he is having abdominal pain at times. He keeps pulling his legs up and grunting. He seems to be straining."

I stood. "Come along, please. We'll examine him together. I'll probably need your help in holding him during the exam."

We entered exam room 4, and Donna went to stand beside Kathy on the other side of the examination table. Edward sat in the corner by my desk, drumming his fingers on the wooden surface. His jaw was rigid, and he wore a scowl on his normally friendly face. It appeared that we had walked in on an argument.

Kathy, petite and attractive, had a few tears trickling down her cheeks taking mascara with them in long lines. She dabbed at her face with a handkerchief in her right hand while stroking little Taylor with her left.

Taylor was quiet, gazing up at the ceiling. He indeed was thin, much too thin for his length and general body habitus. A nearly full bottle of formula beside his little body had apparently just been rejected.

"What's the trouble, folks?" I asked.

Edward eyed me. "What's the trouble indeed? You saw Taylor a month ago and said he was fine. Now look at him."

Kathy gave him a sharp look. "Please don't take offense at Ed. We haven't had much sleep the last two weeks because of Taylor. Ed is not himself today."

Edward folded his arms and looked away from me. "You're right about one thing, Kathy. No sleep."

A few moments of uncomfortable silence ensued. "Ed and Kathy, our goal is to help Taylor, find out what's wrong, and get him the medical attention he needs. Are we agreed?"

She managed a weak smile. "We agree, don't we, Ed?"

After heaving a deep sigh, Ed turned back to me. "Of course you're right. I apologize. It's just been so frustrating watching him suffer."

I decided that he needed to ventilate. "Tell me about it from your standpoint."

Ed stifled a sob. "Taylor won't eat, but he acts starved. Or if he does eat, he gets in a lot of pain. Isn't that right, Kathy?"

"Yes. He takes an ounce or so, then quits and draws his feet up and cries like he's in a lot of distress."

The tense atmosphere in the room vanished as Ed and Kathy talked and affirmed one another's observations. I gave a little sigh of relief myself as I listened to the symptoms they described concerning

Taylor.

Donna pulled a chair over to the examination table so Kathy could sit down. Then she stood beside her, gently resting her hand on Kathy's shoulder.

"How much does Taylor get down in twenty-four hours?" I asked.

Ed nodded at Kathy.

"If we're lucky, maybe twelve ounces a day the last two days," she said. "He seems to be getting worse."

"Does he ever vomit or spit up?"

"He spits up a little, but honestly he gets so little down, I don't see how he could spit up much."

"Has he had other symptoms such as a fever?"

"No. No fever," Ed answered. "I've been checking his temperature a lot."

Kathy smiled at Ed and nodded. "When he says a lot, he's not kidding, Doc. Say every two hours or so for a temp check, and you would come close."

Flushing with embarrassment, Ed leaned forward, clasped his hands together, and looked down at the floor. "I just thought, maybe …"

"That's quite all right," I told him. "I know you and Kathy are good parents. Your other children are well cared for. By the way, have either of them been sick?" Nancy, age seven, and Jordan, age three, were also patients of mine. It had been my privilege to deliver Jordan, but Nancy had been born before I began my medical practice.

Ed still felt the need to talk. He glanced at Kathy and she wisely nodded assent. "No. They're fine. Growing like weeds. I just feel so guilty that Taylor can't seem to improve. Maybe it's my fault?"

"No, Ed, it's definitely not your fault or Kathy's. Now, it is possible that a congenital hereditary condition is to blame, but we don't know that now, and none of us can choose our parents, can we? Do you know if anyone else in the family on either side has had difficulties with what is called failure to thrive in infancy?"

Both Kathy and Ed considered the question, then she spoke. "No. There's nothing like this in either of our families."

I took a few moments to think things through. "How about his bowel movements? I don't recall any particular problems after he was born prior to discharge home."

Kathy thought about that. "The only thing I remember is that the nurses said he was a little delayed. His first bowel movement was two days after birth. And he hasn't been regular like our other children."

"How so?"

"He only moves his bowels every two to four days, and then we have to use a glycerin suppository to help him."

"How many wet diapers does he have in a day?"

"Yesterday, only three slightly wet. Today, only one."

"Are you still bottle- and breast-feeding, Kathy?"

"I gave up breast-feeding. He didn't seem to want my milk either."

"What formula are you using?"

"The same as usual. Similac."

"What you've both told me helps a lot in the differential diagnosis. Now, if you'll allow Donna to assist me, we'll examine Taylor. I hate to disturb him, but we have it to do."

Donna gently restrained Taylor as I did a complete head-to-foot examination. His anterior fontanel was soft with no signs of bulging as in meningitis or brain infection. His mouth was slightly moist, and he seemed eager to suck on the tongue blade briefly. His ears revealed normal tympanic membranes without infection. His heart and lungs checked normal. I carefully auscultated in all quadrants of his abdomen, but when I carefully began to palpate those same areas, he began to fuss and then scream as if in pain. His abdomen was slightly protuberant with firm mass-like effect in the left lower quadrant. I suspected hard stool.

Looking up, I advised that his bowel sounds were a little increased. "If you'll bear with me, I need to carefully do a rectal examination. I believe his colon is not functioning normally."

Both parents stared in wide-eyed alarm. "But he's so little," Ed said. "Is it safe?"

I smiled and nodded. "I've done this examination on younger babies than Taylor. Don't worry. I will only use the tip of my right

25

little finger for the evaluation. I have to know if there is an obstruction."

Ed shrugged.

"It's okay, Doc," Kathy replied. "We trust you to do the right thing. You've always taken good care of our family."

With Donna comforting Taylor and gently restraining him, I did a brief examination and found what I believed to be the problem. Of course, Taylor screamed until Donna picked him up and gently rocked him in her arms.

Taking a seat across from Ed and Kathy, I couldn't help but see the anxiety and fear on their faces. Patients don't always hear what a doctor is telling them, so I began slowly with an explanation of my findings. "Be assured that you've done nothing wrong. In fact, I would say that you've done everything right. You've been doing your best to care for Taylor. He appears to have a distal colonic obstruction just above the anal canal. I'm not worried about it being cancer or anything fatal. Sometimes things go wrong during development in the womb, through no fault of the mother or father. I believe that he could well have a condition called Hirschsprung's disease. It's completely curable but does require a pediatric surgeon to correct the condition. In that disease, the normal neurons that control peristalsis, or movement along the course of the bowel, fail to grow all the way to the end of the last part of the colon. What happens is that stool, or bowel movements, pile up and can only go further with a lot of pressure from above. I don't believe he has extensive disease, because it would have manifested itself much earlier than four months of age."

I proceeded to draw diagrams of the colon for them, particularly the sigmoid colon just above the anal canal, where I believed the deficiency of nerve cells had occurred. He obviously had stool above that area.

Ed looked relieved. "You mean he can be fixed?"

"Yes. If he has Hirschsprung's disease as I suspect, it is entirely curable."

"What now, Doc?"

"With your permission, I'm going to contact Riley Children's Hospital in Indianapolis. They're very good at diagnosing and treating the disease in very young children. They also have top-notch pediatric surgeons skilled in the care of bowel obstructions in children. Whatever the diagnosis of the bowel obstruction, and I really suspect Hirschsprung's, he needs urgent admission. You have done an admirable job of keeping him hydrated under the conditions of his illness, but he needs an IV and extensive laboratory and radiology evaluation to get ahead of this problem."

Donna remained in the room to assist Kathy in changing his diaper and cleaning him up, as the rectal exam had relieved enough stool to make a mess on his little bottom.

Within fifteen minutes, I re-entered the examination room with news that Riley Hospital had accepted him as a patient and a resident doctor would see him on arrival before conferring with a staff physician.

Kathy took my hand. "We really don't know how to thank you. I appreciate your patience with us. We've been under severe stress over Taylor, and I'm afraid it affected our relationship for a while. But that's over now, isn't it, Ed?"

Ed smiled, grasped my hand, and clapped me on the shoulder. "I'm truly sorry for the way I acted when you first came in. I wasn't being nice to Kathy, and I wasn't nice to you either. I appreciate your kindness and extra effort to see that Taylor is cared for."

"Don't you worry about it for one minute," I assured him. "Just get Taylor to Riley tonight and be safe on the way. Remember, you're not an ambulance driver. He needs urgent admission, but you have time to be safe on the way. Your care for him is commendable. I'll look forward to hearing good news from you soon."

Perhaps I was mistaken, but I thought I glimpsed a tear on Ed's cheek. Anyway, I quickly looked the other way.

Now exhausted, I walked the Dixons to the waiting room and then watched out the front window as they drove away, headed for Riley Hospital.

Turning about, I realized Christine and Donna were watching them as well. "Well, ladies, it has been quite a day. But like Christine said, 'not too bad.'"

At that, we all erupted into tension-relieving laughter.

27

***

About three days later, I received a call from the chief resident on the pediatric surgical service at Riley Hospital. I took the call from my wall phone in the lab during office hours.

"Hello, Dr. Matlock. This is Dr. Monroe at Riley Surgical Services. I wish to thank you on behalf of the surgical and pediatric staff for the referral of the nice Dixon family. As you suspected, Taylor had a distal sigmoid colon obstruction due to Hirschsprung's disease. A biopsy confirmed the lack of neurons in the sigmoid, and he had definitive surgery today to remove that small section. The rest of his colon was attached to the anal canal. He did very well, and we expect full recovery. Do you have any questions?"

"No, but thanks much for letting me know. Are the parents doing okay?"

"Yes. They're really nice people. They spoke highly of you and your staff. Thanks again for the referral. We're here for you any time you need us. Have a great day."

"Thanks so much. I always appreciate your help."

When I hung up and turned to resume work, I almost ran into Donna and Christine, who waited expectantly. "I should have known. Nothing in this office escapes either of you."

Christine put her hands on her hips, obviously exasperated, and continued to block my way. "Well, what's the news?"

We all enjoyed a hearty laugh and I relayed the message from Riley Hospital.

Christine was obviously full of joy when she started back to the front office. "As I always say, Doc, this is the healing place."

I could only nod and thank my lucky stars that I had such good help and caring assistants in the practice.

Chapter 4:

Sepsis and Histrionics

"**S**hould we let her come in today?"

Brow furrowed and shaking her head emphatically, Christine stood perplexed in exam room 4 where I sat completing a chart on a patient I had just seen. Exam 4 also doubled as my office and consultation area, where I could escape to write for a few moments when it wasn't occupied by patients, or where I could conduct lengthy discussions with a family when the situation warranted.

I glanced up. "Who?"

"You know who. Our most faithful patient. It's only the fifteenth of the month, and she's already been here three times in two weeks."

"You must be talking about Lydia Isaacs, one of my favorite and most eccentric people in the practice." Lydia was famous for passing out in public places and falling without sustaining injury. She was also a pretty fair actress, having once fooled the hospital nursing staff as she pretended to be paralyzed.

"Well?"

I smiled mischievously. "Well, what?"

Fully frustrated now, Christine tossed her hands in the air. "There are still two hours to go and we're already overbooked at eight patients per hour."

I tried to hide my irritation with Lydia Isaacs while continuing to help Christine evaluate patient complaints. "You know the drill. What are her symptoms today?"

"She says she has a UTI and a fever. But you know Lydia as well as I do. She always says something that she thinks will get her foot in the door."

Sighing, I nodded. "Yes, I know that very well. But did you ask how high her temperature is running?"

"Oh, she said 104. But I never believe her anymore."

"Call her back and tell her to come in."

In her smallest and most pitiful voice, Christine asked, "Really?"

"Yes, really. Remember, even hypochondriacs and drama queens eventually get sick and die. If she is seriously ill this time, that would not reflect well on us now, would it?"

Shrugging, she turned to leave. "I guess not. I just hoped to get out on time for a change. I know you're right. Lydia is just hard to take sometimes."

How well I knew that. Struggling to concentrate, I quickly finished the chart I was working on. Christine was a good soul and loyal employee. I couldn't blame her for the frustration all of us felt.

I tried to pick up the pace so my staff wouldn't be late getting out for a change.

***

Fortunately, those scheduled for the rest of the afternoon were established patients, well known to me and with only minor complaints. With about an hour to go, I was studying results telephoned from the hospital lab regarding my hospitalized patients, when the lab/break room door flew open. Christine and Donna rushed in, closed the door, and burst out laughing.

Donna wiped tears from her eyes as she tried to stifle her laughter. "You will never guess what happened just now."

"I will lay odds that it has something to do with Lydia. Right?"

Christine collapsed into the nearest chair, holding her sides, shaking with laughter. "I'm so glad Lydia came in after all. It was priceless."

The outer office consisted of a spacious waiting area that would comfortably seat about twenty people. Adjacent to the waiting room was the much smaller reception room where Christine worked and about a third of the charts were stored in large metal file cabinets. The ladies could close and lock the reception room door to restrict access, while patients reported at the window where Christine sat answering phones.

It seems that Donna had been pulling charts while Christine talked on the phone. Suddenly, a large pink handkerchief waved right in Christine's face, accompanied by a weak, shaky, disembodied voice coming through the window. "Lydia Isaacs here, girls." Stifling a scream, Christine had spontaneously dropped the phone, rolled her chair backward, and collided with Donna as she was bent over the bottom file drawer, nearly spilling both of them onto the carpet.

Christine jumped up, stuck her head out the window, and was in time to see Lydia all bent over hobbling to a chair in the waiting room, still clutching her colorful handkerchief as soft chuckles erupted around the room. Everyone knew Lydia. It was, as I've said, a small town.

About that time, Matilda Isaacs, Lydia's middle-aged daughter came up to the window. She had been parking the car after letting Lydia out. "Hello, Christine. Has Mother signed in yet?" After a pause, she continued, "My but your face is red. Have you been out in the sun?"

Somehow Christine stammered her way through the sign-in process with Matilda. Meanwhile, Donna busied herself looking the other way, pretending to search through files, doing her best not to laugh. As Matilda took a seat next to her mother, the girls had charged out of the reception room, accompanied by more soft laughter from others waiting to be seen.

After we had a hearty laugh, the girls tried to regain their composure before going back to the outer room. I was just thankful that I didn't have to face those still waiting until a little later.

Serious at last, Christine stood to follow Donna back to the outer office. "You know what? You may have been right. She did look sick today as she took her seat, now that I think about it. I hope she's just looking for attention as usual. I'm going to feel bad if she really is sick."

"I wouldn't worry about it," I said. "No one could blame you for not believing her, whether she is sick or not this time. A patient can only report a certain number of false alarms before people stop believing them, especially with the history of her antics."

***

Fifty minutes later I sat sipping a Diet Coke in the break room while I waited on Lydia to get a urine specimen. Everyone else had been seen and released, mostly colds and flu-type symptoms. However, Lydia had not been able to void earlier. She was last to be seen since she had spent most of the time in the restroom reserved for our patients. Donna had sent Christine home, and we were only thirty minutes past closing time at 5:30 p.m., after seeing fifty patients in the office.

Donna entered the lab with a specimen at last. "You'd better go see Lydia right away. I believe she is really sick this time. Her temp is 104.1, BP 90/60, and pulse 105. Her color is really poor."

"Sure. And if you want, you can go ahead home after you have the urine set up under the microscope. I can lock up and do the night bank deposit. I imagine Christine has it all completed except for this last visit."

"Thanks, but I believe I'll wait. I want to see what you think about her. I've never seen her look this sick before."

Nodding, I hurried down the hall to exam room 3, where the Isaacses waited for me. With a quick glance at the vital signs once more, I entered the room. Lydia was lying on the exam table with a sheet and blanket covering her, visibly shaking from head to foot. Her complexion was an unhealthy grayish color.

"Hello, Lydia. What's the trouble? You seem to be having rigors, severe shaking chills."

Teeth chattering, she tried to answer. "I, I, I don't feel so g-good. I can't quite collect my thoughts." Closing her eyes, she then remained silent, continuing to experience shaking chills.

"Matilda, how long has she been this sick?" I asked. "I believe I saw her a week ago with cold symptoms."

"Yes, and she got a lot better until this morning. She's been acting funny since about noon."

"What do you mean by 'acting funny'?"

"She couldn't remember what we did yesterday or this morning. We visited my cousin yesterday while a neighbor stayed with Dad. He's disabled, you know." Matilda had dedicated her life to caring for her elderly parents.

"When did she start this shaking?"

"About an hour now, more or less."

"Has she complained of anything else?"

"Just of being very hot earlier. Now she says she's very cold."

"Have there been any other symptoms, such as cough, sore throat, headache, back pain, or painful urination?"

"She has had trouble going to the bathroom and said it burned once."

"You mean urination?"

"Yes, trouble getting her urine to flow. But she felt the need to go a lot. Just couldn't go."

I quickly did a head-to-toe general examination, noting poor color, cool and clammy skin with diaphoretic forehead and extremities, lethargic condition, and a weak and rapid pulse as Donna had already noted. She seemed to be quickly deteriorating in front of me. Her lungs were clear, and the heart sounded normal except for the increased rate. There was no abdominal or flank tenderness, and her legs were not swollen or tender.

"Has she been this sick since noon?"

"No. Actually, just since she came back from getting the urine specimen. She was in the bathroom about a half hour. She mentioned feeling a lot worse since then, and her shakes are a lot worse now also. She wasn't this bad when we came in."

"I'll have Donna help you get her dressed while I check the urine, but from all appearances, she likely has urosepsis from the symptoms you described and her general appearance with severe shaking. It's a condition of combined urinary and blood stream infection and is often accompanied by severe rigors like she's having now. She has to go to the hospital immediately for IVs and antibiotics, whatever the etiology of the infection. We'll need to run a battery of tests to be sure of the exact cause of this illness. I'm going to call Art McKay to come at once with the ambulance to take your mother to the hospital. She is seriously ill *this time*."

I hadn't meant to say it that way, but it was too late to take it back. Probably Matilda didn't notice my accidental emphasis on "this time." After all, she never questioned any of her mother's symptoms as being anything but real, no matter whether they made sense or not. Matilda was most definitely not an astute observer of minor details.

Now thoroughly alarmed, she jumped to her feet. "Sure. Whatever you say. Art McKay knows Mom quite well. He has taken her to the hospital many times before."

Muttering now, I said, "I'm sure he has."

As Donna and Matilda helped Lydia get dressed, I put in a call to Art, the local funeral director as well as the owner of the first twenty-four-hour emergency ambulance service for Glen Oaks and the surrounding countryside. Afterward, reviewing the microscopic findings, I noted multiple clumps of WBCs with likely bacterial rods present. The dipstick revealed positive results for protein, nitrite, and leukocyte esterase, all findings consistent with infection.

I was relaying the findings to Matilda and her mother when Art McKay pulled into the parking lot with siren going full blast and red lights flashing in strobe-like fashion, weirdly illuminating the office interior through the large picture window in the waiting room. Evening shadows were falling as Donna held the door open and Art came struggling in pulling the front of the gurney while Ollie Stone, a talkative EMT, guided the back of the cart through the door but allowed Art to do most of the work.

Poor Art, obese and out of condition, was already huffing and puffing, red-faced, sweating, and short of breath from the exertion. Ollie remained all smiles as he followed him down the hallway to the exam room, never offering to even assist as Art pulled the gurney unaided. Ollie wasn't really lazy, just a little mentally challenged, one might say.

With our assistance, Lydia was finally safely belted to the

gurney, covered with blankets, and headed out the door. Ollie again brought up the rear, this time with his hands at least steadying the cart while Art tugged it along. I didn't try to interfere or help. Art always said he wanted Ollie to learn on his own.

Willie Robertson, a reliable middle-aged EMT, then roared into the gravel lot in a cloud of dust, blue emergency lights flashing on his vehicle, arriving just in time to park his 1960 Chevy pickup in our lot and assist with the transport to the hospital at Glen Falls. I'm sure Art was glad to see him.

Ollie climbed into the front passenger seat while Willie got in the back to ride with Lydia and monitor her vital signs, then he waved and called out loudly in his sing-song voice, "See y'all later. I just love this kind of work. I strongly admire helpin' folks in need."

Donna secured the office for the night, and I stepped into the break room and dialed the hospital operator. Within moments she had the evening house supervisor on the line.

Ann Kilgore's pleasant, authoritative voice came over the line. "Hello, Dr. Matlock. What do you have for us tonight?"

"Good evening, Ann. I just sent Art McKay and the boys with Lydia Isaacs for admission. I hope we still have some beds."

Ann laughed. "Really, Doc. Did she need to come by ambulance again?"

"I know what you're thinking, but this time Lydia really is desperately ill. She has urosepsis and borderline shock. Your staff will need to work quickly to get her started on IVs and antibiotics."

Ann finally composed herself. "This had better be the real thing and not another faked illness. You'll have a hard time living it down if it's another one of her usual escapades."

I provided her vital signs, physical exam findings, and UA results while Ann listened.

"It sure sounds like the real deal this time," she agreed. "What orders do you want me to start with?"

Rapid-fire, I gave orders for urine culture and sensitivity, blood cultures x 2, IV fluids with a 500 ml bolus of normal saline to be followed by normal saline at 150 ml per hour, IV gentamicin and cephalexin with daily labs, and stat labs on admission including electrolytes, BUN, creatinine, and CBC. Chest X-ray and EKG were to be done immediately along with the usual general comfort orders including acetaminophen for fever control.

"Anything else?"

"Only that I'll be in—"

"I know. Never mind. You'll be in to check on her in a little while, right?"

"Right you are."

Ann laughed pleasantly. "Then I'll see you in a little while. Don't come too soon or you'll beat Art and the boys here." Ann was also a resident of Glen Oaks, so she knew Art and his crew of loveable EMTs quite well. They never got anywhere rapidly despite their flashing lights and sirens, but they could always be counted on to show up eventually.

***

Lydia Isaacs made a rapid recovery in the hospital. Her blood pressure, pulse, and temperature rapidly normalized and her mentation returned to normal. She received IV antibiotics for ten days, and the urine was proven to be completely clear from the seventh day. She had experienced *E. coli* sepsis, one of the types of Gram-negative septicemia due to a common coliform bacteria. These bacteria dye red in the Gram stain test, thus are called Gram-negative. Most types of *E. coli* are normally harmless, even beneficial if they remain in the colon, but they can be deadly when invading the urinary tract.

I planned to discharge Lydia back home on day twelve, after she was off antibiotics for twenty-four hours. In the 1970s, doctors had no pressure to discharge patients home before recovery from a serious illness, and I wanted to be sure her infection wouldn't return with a vengeance.

On a cool, breezy morning, I left my car in the physician's parking lot at the south side of the hospital to make my way to the medical floor. Ann Kilgore was just getting off work and had punched the time clock at 7:00 a.m. before exiting the building.

Smiling broadly, she greeted me, "You'll never guess what I saw last night."

Instinctively, I knew something big was coming. "No, I can't guess, but I'm sure you're going to relish telling me all about it."

"You are so right. You made a mistake yesterday during rounds."

Now taken aback, I began to wrack my brain for what embarrassing mistake I might have made. All the while, she watched me with a silly grin on her face.

"Okay. You've got me," I said. "What did I do?"

"You told Lydia that she's going home today." She had assumed an accusing tone of voice as she continued enjoying my evident misery. "Didn't you?"

"Yes. What did she do?"

"About midnight I was passing by her doorway when I noticed her grunting and moving about in bed. I stopped to watch just as she climbed out over the rail, got down in the floor, pillow under her head of course, and started to yell for help."

"You have to be kidding me. What did you do?"

"I simply cleared my throat, assumed my meanest voice, and said, 'I watched you climb out of that bed and get down on the floor. Now you can just get back in the same way you got out.'"

I laughed. "Wow. I guess I shouldn't have told her about going home."

"Don't worry, Doc. She'll go home all right. Even Lydia is sensitive enough to occasionally get embarrassed. She asked me not to tell you, but I made her no promises. I think you're safe. You won't even need to mention it to her." She started for the door, but then turned around. "Have a really great day. And could you please keep Lydia home for at least a couple of weeks?" With that, she left still laughing.

When I saw Lydia, I made a point not to mention her latest antics, but I did ask a few pertinent questions before signing her release. "Tell me, Lydia, how was your night?"

She eyed me suspiciously for several seconds before clearing her throat to answer. "Well, I slept pretty good. Nothing much happened. Why?"

"Oh, I just thought I'd ask. Routine, you know."

"Why, sure. Just routine, and I'm ready to go home." Lydia

sighed wistfully while looking about the room before concluding, "At least I guess I am."

Chapter 5:

Febrile Illness in a Teenager

"**D**octor, I've never seen Tiffany so lifeless and sick. She sleeps most of the time. Can you help us?"

The anxious, desperate mother, Mary Ann Ballard, sat in the chair at the head of the examination table where her oldest daughter reclined listlessly, eyes closed, face flushed, pigtails in sharp contrast to the white sheet and pillowcase.

Glancing back at Mary Ann, I noted the striking resemblance between mother and daughter: auburn hair, medium build, striking good looks, and refined facial features. "Can you start at the beginning and tell me more about her illness?"

"Yes, of course." College educated and articulate, Mary Ann began her narration. "She has been ill for three days now, started out with a low-grade fever. I didn't think much about it in the beginning. With four red-headed daughters, it seems like someone is always sick with a URI or some type of flu. But this is different from what the girls usually experience. Despite multiple childhood illnesses, they always bounce back quickly."

After pausing to blot a tear with a delicate handkerchief, she resumed, "Tiffany just gets progressively worse. First day, temperature 100, yesterday 103, today 104.2. She is so very lethargic now that it frightens me. My husband and I are dreadfully worried.

Brad is out of town on business, but he advised me to get her here at once."

"What about other symptoms?"

"It's mostly just what I've told you, fever and lethargy. She hasn't been coughing or sniffling. I asked her about diarrhea and vomiting. None so far. No UTI symptoms and she's never had a urinary tract infection."

"Is she having normal periods and when was her last?"

"Two weeks ago and no problems other than the usual cramps. And no, Doctor. I know what you're thinking. She's not sexually active. We've taught her the importance of waiting for the right young man to come into her life. She's a very conscientious and obedient child. She has no boyfriends at present." She chuckled. "Brad has scared them all off. He gruffly tells them she has to be sixteen before she can have a chaperoned date. One look at his scowling face, and they quickly recall the need to be elsewhere."

I smiled. "Good. Far too many young girls have little guidance in such matters these days. I'm sorry to say that I've delivered thirteen- and fourteen-year-old girls with no preparation for being mothers. Now, has anyone else been ill at home? Has she had any overnight stays with girlfriends who might be ill now?"

"No. No overnight pajama parties. Frances, our youngest, recently had the sniffles, but no such fever or prostration as Tiffany has experienced. Julia and Rachel are just fine, hyperactive and twittering worse than a flock of starlings all day long."

"Anything else unusual—accidents, minor cuts or abrasions, vaccinations at the public health office?"

"No. No recent vaccinations and nothing else I can think of offhand."

I nodded. "She hasn't complained of headaches, dizziness, or visual problems?"

"Oh, she had a slight headache, but nothing major. And it didn't last long."

"How about any tick, spider, or mosquito bites?"

"Nothing at all."

I moved to Tiffany's side and rested my right hand on her left shoulder. Her deep blue eyes fluttered open and she managed a weak smile, nodded slightly, and mouthed, "Hello."

"I understand that you've been quite a sick young lady."

Weakly nodding, she closed her eyes again.

"Does the light hurt your eyes?"

Opening her eyes quickly, she looked directly at me. "No, not really. I just feel so weak and tired. If you could raise the head of the table, I believe it would help a little."

"Sure thing." I brought her head up to about thirty-five degrees elevation by raising the top of the examination table. "How's that?"

"Better."

"I'm going to examine you as usual, Tiffany. Please let me know if anything I do during the examination causes you to be in pain." Carefully lifting her head to flex her neck, I asked, "Does that hurt at all?"

"No, not at all."

"Good. Can you tell me your age, birthday, and home address?"

Smiling now, she answered, "Of course I can," whereupon she proceeded to give all of the appropriate answers. I watched her mother to be sure of the factual authenticity.

Mrs. Ballard nodded in affirmation before I continued the usual head-to-toe general examination.

Face and cheeks still flushed. Cranial nerves and sensorium all normal. No evidence of URI. Lungs clear. Heart with regular rate and rhythm plus a soft 2/6 systolic ejection murmur. Abdomen soft and nontender. Extremities somewhat pale, but complexion very fair normally. No skin or nail lesions noted. Reflexes in the extremities all normally reactive. Other than fever, lethargy, and a soft heart murmur, the findings were all within normal limits.

Somewhat puzzled, I resumed my seat. "The only abnormal findings are fever, lethargy, and a soft heart murmur, one her former physician documented according to her old records. It was thought to be an innocent murmur of childhood that would likely disappear as she grows older. Many children have them. It's probably not relevant to her illness. She appears to have a systemic infection such as a severe viral or bacterial illness, but I can't find any definite source."

Glancing down at the completely normal urine dipstick that Donna had handed me before the examination, I continued, "There's no sign of serious brain or nervous system infection, no recent vaccinations, no UTI symptoms or signs, nothing specific at all. Vital signs checked by Donna were within normal limits, except for her temperature. Yet she is quite ill. I believe she should be hospitalized and have a battery of tests, such as blood cultures and chest X-ray, as well as general observation to determine and treat the source if it happens to be bacterial. Hopefully it's viral and will soon run its course."

"That would be fine with me. Brad and I were hoping you would put her in the hospital for testing. He won't be home before tomorrow evening from his business trip, and I know he would rest easier with her in the hospital. The high fever frightens us when it continues even with ibuprofen and acetaminophen."

"One more thing. I've seen her twice in the past and noted the heart murmur documented in the medical record you brought with you when Brad's work transferred him to Glen Falls. Was there ever any thought that she might have had rheumatic fever in the past?"

"No. Dr. Redmon in Ohio said it should be watched but would likely disappear. She has been so healthy, he never really worried about it."

Soon the Ballard family was en route to the hospital at Glen Falls while I finished seeing my other patients. On my way home, I had the uncomfortable feeling that I was missing something. I hoped that the laboratory testing would reveal the source of infection, if that was indeed her problem. I fretted because some serious autoimmune diseases and blood diseases can start in similar fashion. I desperately hoped she didn't have one of the acute childhood leukemias.

***

Following a late dinner with my wife and children, I slowly drove the backroads to the hospital in Glen Falls. The scenic drive through farm country always relaxed me, and I wanted time to think about the possible etiology of Tiffany's ailment. I was haunted by the feeling that she had a very serious illness.

At the hospital I slowly climbed the stairway to the second floor, avoiding the elevator, still wanting time to mentally review the findings. Lab work should be coming back anytime now. (In the 1970s, however, our laboratory armamentarium was much more limited.)

Arriving on the 2 South Medical Floor, I was greeted by Ann Kilgore, the evening supervisor. "Doc, you sure have one sick little girl in room 220. Have you seen any of her labs yet?"

"No, that's why I'm here now. What do you have so far?"

"I left her chart with her floor nurse, Hannah Carter. She's finishing her admission charting. She has the labs that are just coming back."

"Thanks, Ann." I hurried to the chart room to review the tests.

"Good evening," Hannah said. "Here's your chart. I'm anxious to know what you think." She stood nearby as I perused the chart and laboratory findings.

With increasing concern, I shook my head, pondering the results:

1. WBC: 21,000 with 95% polymorphonucleocytes and 5% lymphocytes.

2. Hemoglobin/hematocrit normal at 12.0 and 36.4.

3. RBC morphology noted to be normal by the automated lab machine.

4. Platelets normal.

5. BUN slightly elevated at 25 with creatinine of 1.0.

6. Blood cultures x 2 and throat culture pending.

7. ASO titer normal.

8. Sed rate elevated at 40.

9. Antinuclear antibody and LE tests for lupus pending.

10. EKG: No official reading, but I concluded that it was completely normal. In those days, I was one of three official EKG readers at our hospital since I had the benefit of several months of EKG reading during training and had demonstrated satisfactory expertise on testing.

Impatient now, Hannah asked, "What do you think? It looks like an infection to me, but where is it coming from?" As an experienced middle-aged floor nurse who had taken care of a lot of children in her twenty years of nursing, she was also worried.

"I wish I knew. But she appears to be septic with a likely bacterial infection and mild dehydration. Did you get a urine to recheck my office findings yet?"

"Sent it to the lab five minutes ago."

"Has her chest X-ray been taken?"

"She had it completed before coming to the floor. Unfortunately, the radiologist had already gone home. No reading yet."

"How about her temperature?"

"We got it down to 99.8, but it's already going back up less than an hour later."

"Were you able to start her IV? It looked to me like she might be a difficult stick."

With a smug look on her face, Hannah answered proudly, "I've been doing this a long time. I got the IV on the first stick. Her IV fluids are running at 100 ml per hour, just like you ordered."

"I'm going to go downstairs to review the chest X-ray and see if the UA is completed yet. Is the family still here?"

"Her mother is spending the night with us. I fixed her up with a recliner and some warm blankets. She sent the other three girls home with her mother and dad. I have to confess, I let the younger sisters peek in from the doorway and wave at them. Don't tell on me."

I chuckled and turned to make my way down to the main floor where the lab and radiology departments were located. "Don't worry. I didn't see anything."

After confirming that the UA results in the lab were normal, I went across the hall to the radiology department, where Sally Walker, the twenty-two-year-old evening radiology technician, greeted me.

Methodical, conscientious, and anxious to please the staff, she motioned for me to follow her to the reading room. "I knew you would be in to look at these. I was just getting the evening films ready for the radiologist to review in the morning, but I left yours up on the view box in here."

Sally returned to her work as I studied the two-view chest X-ray, PA and lateral standard views. The PA (postero-anterior) was taken from the back side of the patient with them sitting or standing facing the X-ray film. The lateral was taken from the side of the patient. I had quite a lot of experience looking at X-rays already but could find nothing abnormal on those films. I returned to the medical floor to examine Tiffany one last time, anxious to know how the radiologist would read them in the morning.

With an undetermined source of fever, Tiffany had been placed in a private room with glove and gown precautions for infection control, so after donning the proper attire, I entered her room. She was asleep, so I nodded to Mrs. Ballard and carefully slipped my stethoscope onto Tiffany's chest, listening through the hospital gown. Once again I found clear lung sounds on both sides of the chest, regular heart rate and rhythm of 95, and a grade 2/6 systolic ejection murmur. Studying her features as I auscultated the heart sounds, I noted flushed face but no evidence of cyanosis of her lips.

I quietly removed my gloves and gown and motioned for Mrs. Ballard to follow me to the door, where I scrubbed my hands once more after placing the mask in the trash can and the yellow gown in the red plastic bin labeled *Contaminated Laundry*.

"Her white blood count indicates a likely bacterial infection. Her chest X-ray and EKG are normal. I can't find a source yet, but cultures have been taken and I plan to start IV cephalexin. She's mildly dehydrated with elevated BUN but normal creatinine, both renal function tests that also indicate state of hydration. Her red blood count is normal with no sign of anemia. Platelets are also normal. She doesn't appear to have any coagulation problems."

When she nodded, I continued, "I have an ASO titer and throat culture checking for strep infection pending. Also, some immune tests will take a while to complete, but they will likely be negative. This looks more like an acute infection. That's why I'm starting antibiotics empirically tonight." (In those days, cephalexin—brand name Keflex—was a fairly new, powerful antibiotic used in a wide variety of conditions both orally and intravenously. With ongoing bacterial resistance, it has since lost much of its effectiveness.)

Mrs. Ballard appeared relieved that at least no more serious diagnoses had been made. "I'm sure you know best. Do whatever you think is right."

"One more thing. Since her fever continues to spike, I'm going to leave orders for the lab to draw blood cultures for any temperature of 101.5 or greater. Sometimes we find bacteria in the blood stream during sudden spikes in fever."

I headed home then, and glancing at my watch as I left the parking lot, I realized that it was already 10:18 p.m. Still concerned, I fell into bed exhausted about 11:30, setting my alarm for 6:00 a.m. before turning off the bedside lamp.

Tomorrow would bring more answers.

Chapter 6:

Subtle Congenital Heart Disease

As I sipped my coffee on the drive to work the next morning, I continued to think about Tiffany Ballard and her apparent infection. I had received no phone calls during the night regarding her condition, so she had to be at least stable. A favorable sign, I hoped.

At the hospital I walked into the doctor's lounge and flipped on my light, indicating to the operator that I was available. A note to call the switchboard on arrival awaited me, so I did that. "Hello, Rose. This is Dr. Matlock. Do you have a message for me?"

Rose Adams, a sixty-one-year-old woman with a pleasant voice came on the line. "Yes. You're to call Mike in the lab right away. I'll be glad to ring you through."

After a short pause, Mike Curry, the chief lab technician as well as head of the lab, answered. His deep bass voice reverberated over the line. "Dr. Matlock. It's about your patient Tiffany Ballard."

"Yes?"

"Her first two blood cultures from last night are already growing out bacteria, and it looks like *Staphylococcus aureus*. She's had four other cultures since those on admission for temp spikes, and the first one of those is already showing growth. Does she have an obvious abscess or skin wound, and do you want us to keep doing blood cultures for temps?"

"No. No obvious wounds or abscesses. It's a mystifying case so far, but she does have a heart murmur. Maybe she has bacterial endocarditis. Just do one more culture if her fever goes back up again."

"The reason I asked is that the phlebotomist is on the way back to the medical floor. Temp's already back up."

"Sure. You can stop after this next set of cultures. I'll write the order to discontinue them right away."

"Okay, Doc. If you need any more, you only have to give us a call. Thanks a lot. I hate to have to keep sticking this young girl if we have enough data already."

"I agree, Mike. Thanks for letting me know."

***

Mere minutes later, I was once again in room 220 with Tiffany and her mother. Another careful examination showed no obvious portal of entry for a bacterial infection.

Tiffany was awake and alert after her seventh set of blood cultures since admission. "Do I have to have more blood tests today? My arms are getting sore."

"No, probably not, Tiffany. We're getting some answers now." I turned to Mrs. Ballard. "It looks like she has a blood stream infection, possibly with a staph-type bacterium. I'm wondering if she's had any minor wounds or abrasions in the last week or so."

"Not that I can think of. Unless … surely a simple dental procedure wouldn't cause sufficient injury to lead to infection, would it?"

"What kind of dental procedure?"

"I took her to have her teeth cleaned a week ago yesterday. She's had routine cleanings every six months for several years now with no previous problems. Surely you don't think—"

"What about the heart murmur? Has she ever taken prophylactic antibiotics prior to minor dental procedures in the past?"

"No. We were told that it appeared to be a normal innocent heart murmur that she would outgrow. No one ever recommended antibiotics before dental cleaning or anything else."

I considered that. "Obviously, now I'm concerned about the

possibility of a cardiac infection. With your permission, I'd like to call in a cardiologist for consultation. Dr. Alan Hill practices in Indianapolis at IU Medical Center and other area hospitals. He's an excellent physician, and I would like his input for her care."

"Yes, of course. Please call him as soon as you can."

"He may want to transfer her to an Indianapolis hospital. I assume that would be okay with you?"

"Certainly."

"I'll be right back."

Within twenty minutes, I had Alan Hill on the line. He had been one of my mentors at IU School of Medicine. "What's up, Carl?" he asked. "Is there someone you would like me to see?"

"Yes. Let me give you a brief history." I gave him a quick summary of Tiffany's illness, then awaited his response.

"I'm out of the office today and just finished with rounds," he said. "I don't have anything else on the schedule. How would you like me to come to your hospital to see her later this morning?"

"That would be great. I'll see the chief of medicine and get you temporary credentials for consultation in-house here. The staff is familiar with you after your presentation to our county medical society a couple of months ago. I'm sure it'll be no problem. Give me a few minutes and I'll get back with you."

***

With his consulting credentials readily approved by the chief of medicine and seconded by the chief of staff, Alan Hill was soon at the bedside. I had rescheduled my earliest office patients in order to be present for his evaluation. Brad Ballard had taken an early flight home, and both he and Mary Ann were present for the consultation.

Alan Hill was a doctor's doctor—well groomed, eloquent, highly professional, and neatly attired in a dark blue suit with white shirt and matching blue tie. He carried out a very thorough examination of Tiffany after putting her at ease with his pleasance. He was a handsome man, and Tiffany perked up, obviously flattered by his interest and gentle manner.

He pointed out a few tiny recently formed splinter-like

hemorrhages in her nail beds, then proceeded with his examination. Finally, he asked the nurse to bring him a pad and pencil from the nurses' station.

With the Bradleys and me hanging on his every word, he explained the problem as he drew a diagram of the heart.[1] Dr. Matlock has done an excellent job of making an initial diagnosis. She now has several positive cultures of *Staphylococcal aureus* growing in the lab. She has endocarditis with a blood stream infection. These little splinter hemorrhages are manifestations of the infection, but they'll resolve eventually with treatment. She's receiving an antibiotic that has a favorable profile for treatment, but I believe an even better choice is a drug called methicillin a very potent anti-staphylococcal antibiotic, currently the drug of choice until something better comes along."

He looked up from his drawing. "She has a blood stream infection, in all probability related to her dental procedure. Even minor dental procedures are known to cause transient bacteremia or blood stream invasion. When that happens, if there's an abnormal area of turbulence in the heart, such as a defective valve or a closure defect in the upper or lower wall of the heart, then bacteria can take up residence and cause a severe infection."

He started drawing again, this time illustrating the problem by drawing four chambers, two upper and two lower. "This is not anatomically correct, just a simple drawing to illustrate what's going on. We physicians usually check people from the front, so the left chambers are on your right with the right chambers on your left. The right heart receives poorly oxygenated blood from the body and is normally a low-pressure, volume pump, as the flow of blood is continuously returned from the body to the right heart to replenish the oxygen supply in the lungs. The main function of the right heart is to pump all that blood to the lungs.

"The left heart is a pressure pump, receiving oxygen rich blood from the lungs and sending it out to the entire body. Each

---

[1] See the diagram of atrial septal defect following this chapter, simply drawn to explain the mechanics of the defect. I have used this approach many times with patients. Note that it looks very different anatomically.

beat, or systole, pumps more blood. Each rest between times, or diastole, allows the heart to fill with blood on both sides at once. Now, back to the four chambers. There are two on the right, an upper called the right atrium, and a lower called the right ventricle. On the left we have correspondingly an upper left atrium and a lower left ventricle. There are four heart valves, one on each side between the upper and lower chambers, and one on each side at the outlet of the ventricles.

"Bacteria can settle on heart valves, but they can also settle on abnormal openings in the wall, or septum, between the upper atria, or the septum between the lower ventricles, thus making possible leaks from left to right, and in severe cases, from right to left. Left to right is the early stage where it flows from the high-pressure left side to the low-pressure right side."

"Do you mean to say that she has an infection in her heart, probably from having her teeth cleaned?" Mr. Ballard interrupted. "And that her heart valves are affected?"

"Yes, that's exactly what I'm saying, except that I don't believe it's the valves that are problematic. Tiffany has the classic murmur of atrial septal defect of the ostium secundum type, but the type isn't really pertinent to our discussion just now. The important thing is that she has a very small hole between the upper chambers of her heart. This never closed as she developed in the womb or in early infancy and still continues as she developed into a young lady, and that's the problem."

He looked from Brad to Mary Ann. "The interesting thing is that many people have these abnormalities, and as long as they're small, they may lead a relatively normal life and never have the ASD, or atrial septal defect, diagnosed. These abnormalities are not such that with small defects between the atria, we would even think of prophylactic antibiotics. They usually don't get infected with dental procedures. But, and it's a big *but*, in medicine and in life there are exceptions to just about every rule."

"How can you be so sure that it's a small opening between the upper chambers?" Kathy asked. "I don't doubt your ability. I'm just a worried mother."

Dr. Hill smiled and nodded. "I don't blame you for being

anxious. I would only wonder about you if you weren't."

Tiffany laughed softly, and her parents smiled at one another, visibly relaxing. "Please continue, Dr. Hill. This is very interesting. Mom and Dad will catch up with you, so go on. I've always been interested in nursing. Maybe that's what I'll do someday."

"Maybe you will, Tiffany," he agreed. "Now, where did I leave off?"

"You were telling about my ASD, I think you called it."

"Right. When the defect is small, especially when it stays small, there's a small amount of passage of oxygenated blood from the left upper chamber—or left atrium—into the right upper chamber—or right atrium—from an area of higher pressure to an area of lower pressure. This blood is already oxygenated, small in quantity, and causes no major problems, sometimes for years, sometimes apparently for a lifetime.

"However, the defect can cause problems if it's very large or if something causes the pressure to rise much higher on the right side and reverses the flow. But that's not at all what we're dealing with here. As to how I can be so certain, there are a couple of reasons. First, the main murmur is relatively soft, grade 2/6, what we call a systolic ejection murmur. It occurs during systole, or when the heart pumps. The increased flow into the right atrium increases the blood flowing across the outlet valve of the right ventricle—the pulmonic valve—enough to cause a flow disturbance resulting in the sound we hear. It's a short crescendo-decrescendo murmur, very typical of ASD.

"Second, there is fixed splitting of S2, the second heart sound, meaning it's unaffected by respiration. The second heart sound results from closure of both exit valves from the lower chambers, the ventricles, aortic and pulmonic. In expiration, they normally create a single sound, what we might call a single S2. That is the *dub* sound, as in *lub-dub*. In ASD, there is enough increased volume of blood on the right side to delay closure of the pulmonic valve on the right. Thus, you have something that sounds like *lub-dub-dub*, a split S2. During normal respiration with a normal heart, the pressure changes in the chest cavity cause increased flow and a temporarily split S2 with inspiration. Normal expiration decreases blood return, decreases blood going through the right heart, and the sound should be single, a single *dub* so to speak.

"Further confusing this for laymen, the valve separating the right upper and lower chambers—the tricuspid valve—flutters more due to increased amounts of blood passing from the right atrium to the right ventricle during the rest, or filling, phase of the heart called diastole. This causes a very soft low-pitched diastolic rumble-type murmur at the lower left sternal area. But it's difficult to hear. You have to have good hearing, a good stethoscope, and know just where to listen to even find it. I've been specially trained to suspect it when I hear a fixed split S2 sound, as I already related. It's part of my job. Is everyone thoroughly confused now?"

The Ballards smiled and nodded.

"I was afraid of that. Let me try to briefly summarize. Tiffany has a very small hole between the upper chambers of her heart—an atrial septal defect. She was born with it. Bacteria have settled on that area of the heart by some unusual chance occurrence, resulting from the blood stream invasion during her minor dental procedure. It's a one-off rare event, but a potentially serious one at that. The blood in the left atrium is adding increased volume to the right atrium with every beat. This would likely not have been discovered for years without this infection. But this murmur she has is due to increased blood flow vibrating the pulmonic valve of the right ventricle as blood flows out en route to the lungs for oxygen during the systolic phase. Also, the tricuspid valve between the upper right atrium and lower right ventricle vibrates during the relaxation phase of diastole, as the lower chamber fills back up. That murmur is extremely hard to hear. Even cardiologists miss it at times."

Dr. Hill smiled at Tiffany as he took her hands in his, gave them a gentle squeeze, and asked, "Do you understand most of what I said and tried to crudely illustrate for you?"

Clearly excited and pleased now, Tiffany said, "Dr. Hill, I do get it. You and Dr. Matlock are going to help me get well now. I just know that you will."

"Tiffany, I'm going to suggest that Dr. Matlock keep you here, close to your parents' home where it won't be as much of a hardship for them to visit with you. I'll be happy to make the trip from Indianapolis every day or two to see you and help monitor your progress. It's only about twenty minutes from my home via the interstate. It takes me that long or longer to get to downtown Indy during rush hour. There isn't much to do now but give at least six weeks of IV antibiotics, monitor frequent blood and urine tests, and wait for you to recover. If we're all agreed, we will proceed with that plan."

"It's fine with us," Brad answered for the family. "As long as you're both watching her, I'm comfortable with that approach. But what about the ASD? Will it need to be fixed later?"

"That's a good question. It's very likely that it will require closure, but that will be delayed until she's completely well. A cardiac catheterization is usually done first, and a surgical cardiovascular team will be consulted for definitive closure when she has recovered her usual good health."

After the consultation, Dr. Hill and I retired to the doctors' chart room to speak privately. "She's a fortunate young lady. I'm certain the ASD is the problem," he told me. "She has no decompensation in cardiovascular status and should do well. You can call me at any time, day or night, if you have any questions regarding her condition. I'm also leaving my emergency contact number here with the nursing staff. In the unlikely circumstance that she should deteriorate, I'll immediately arrange for an ICU bed in one of the Indianapolis hospitals. It's very unusual for an ASD to become infected following a dental procedure. Some of these defects are only discovered incidentally at autopsy after a normal lifetime and death from other causes."

I nodded. "Thanks a lot for your help. I know the Ballards appreciate it, and so do I."

He clapped me on the shoulder. "Anytime, Carl. I'm always glad to help."

***

Medicine was practiced in a very different environment in the 1970s. I don't believe bacterial endocarditis would ever be treated in a small county hospital in today's litigious society, with the possible exception of a remote wilderness area with internet video consultation available.

I'm glad to say that Tiffany recovered and had definitive correction at a later date with no complications. The last time I saw her, several years ago, she was in excellent health.

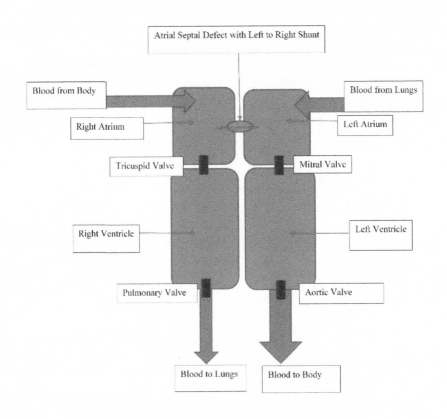

Chapter 7:

Fishermen's Tales

Johnny Morton loved to fish, but his many misadventures made him a regular visitor in the office. Just turned seventeen years old, he was a senior student and the starting tackle on the local high school football team, and he had the husky build to match. Johnny stood five feet six inches tall in his socks and sported an unruly shock of dark brown hair complementing his deep brown eyes. He lived for summer vacations, when he could spend his days on local farm ponds and lakes with his trusty Shakespeare seven-foot spinning rod and reel outfit.

Nearing the end of a typical day in early summer, I sat in my office writing quickly, trying my best to get out on time. I had seen forty-five patients and was ready to go home. Christine was emptying trash cans into large plastic bags as I put the finishing touches on the last chart. Sighing in relief, I gathered my notes to be placed in the proper charts, but that could wait until morning.

Donna entered my office with a look of exasperation marring her usually pleasant countenance. "Dr. Matlock, I'm afraid you're not through yet. Johnny Morton just came in the door."

I shook my head, anxious to go home. "What has he done now? Can't it wait until tomorrow?"

She smiled grimly. "You be the judge. Just follow me."

I felt all the energy drain from my body. "This is the one night I really didn't want to be late getting home. We planned to take the kids out to the city park playground in Glen Falls and then eat at

Dairy Queen. They're looking forward to it."

After following Donna into exam room 1, I stopped in amazement. "I thought you said *Johnny* Morton was here to be seen."

"I didn't say he was to be seen," she corrected. "I said he was here, and he is."

Seated in the room, tears freely flowing down her cheeks, sat Tammy Morton, Johnny's eleven-year-old sister. Protruding from her bloody lower lip was a large fishhook. The front of her blue sweater was stained with fresh blood.

Johnny came in from the hallway just then. "Hi, Doc. I guess you could say that this is the big one that got away."

Tammy glared at Johnny, and he ducked his head. "Sorry, Sis. Just trying to be funny. Wanted to cheer you up."

"How in the world did you hook your sister?" I asked.

"It was like this. I had my rod and reel leaning against the wall in the hallway. Our pup ran into the pole and knocked it over as Tammy lunged for him. Well, you can see for yourself what happened next."

I tried not to reveal my disgust. "Do you always store your fishing pole with the hooks still attached in prominent locations in your home?"

"Yeah, I guess so." Johnny's face fell again and he resumed studying his feet. "Ma said it was all my fault. She made me come ahead with Tammy. Said I was responsible for the bill. I don't think she has gotten over one of my hooks tearing a big rip in Dad's new work pants last week."

I nodded. "Well, Donna, I guess we'd better get this fixed."

Embarrassed, Johnny felt the need to talk. "Ma will be here in a few minutes. She was just finishing our supper and had some rolls to take out of the oven."

"It's okay, Johnny. Just have a seat. As I recall, you don't do well with the sight of needles and blood. I don't want you passing out again."

Donna had anticipated exactly what I needed to remove the hook and care for Tammy. While I made sure Johnny was seated, she prepared Tammy by having her lie supine on the exam table and gently cleansed her mouth and lower face with sterile saline, sponging up the excess with sterilized towels from our autoclave. Donna then arranged fresh towels over Tammy's lower face, leaving her eyes uncovered so she would be less frightened. She moved to the other side of the table and took Tammy's hand as I donned sterile gloves.

Christine wheeled in the sterile instruments on the tray Donna had prepared before entering the room, then saw the embedded hook and paled. "I'd stay and help, but I don't do well watching surgery." She hurried from the room.

I opened the sterile pack and drew up 1% lidocaine with epinephrine using an 18-gauge needle and 3 ml syringe. The lidocaine would provide topical anesthesia while the epinephrine would inhibit bleeding.

Tammy's eyes grew wide with alarm.

"Don't worry," I said. "I'm switching to a very small needle to inject the medication. It works very fast and you'll feel very little after the medicine is injected." I continued to talk, mostly to hopefully keep Tammy calm. "This medicine will also keep you from bleeding much. I use it in highly vascular areas with abundant circulation. I don't use epinephrine on fingers or toes, too much risk of poor blood flow right afterward. Epinephrine is another name for adrenaline. Maybe you've studied it in school, the fight or flight hormone. I won't inject much to remove the hook, so you probably won't feel any side effects from the medication. Just numbness for a little while."

Tammy made a fleeting attempt to smile, then shut her eyes tight and gripped Donna's hand tightly.

I quickly injected about 1.5 ml into and about the puncture wound. "That's all there is to it. You'll not have any pain while I remove the hook."

Tammy opened her eyes, loosened her grip on Donna's hand, and shuddered briefly.

Glancing at Johnny sitting in the corner, I noticed that he had picked up one of the office magazines, *Sports Afield*. It had a special fishing section that he pretended to be reading, but he looked a little on the green side. "Do you need to go out to the waiting room while I finish with your sister?"

Johnny stood up. "Maybe I should. She might feel better if I didn't watch." He left the room in a hurry.

Using a small hemostat to grip and steady the shank of the hook, I made a 1-millimeter incision over the buried sharp barb. I gently pushed the barb and sharp pointed end on through the lip, careful not to cause further damage, then cut off the barb and point with a special small metal cutter. Finally, I backed the rest of the hook out of the wound through the same track it had followed on initial penetration of the lower lip. "All finished, Tammy. There's very little bleeding, but I'm going to apply a little pressure on the moist gauze I have over the wound for a minute or two."

Visibly relaxed, she smiled first at Donna, then at me.

In a short time, Donna had cleansed the wound with more sterile saline and gave Tammy a moistened gauze to hold gently on the wound for the next several minutes.

By the time we were finished, Mrs. Morton was there to retrieve her children. "I don't know what I'm going to do with Johnny. He's so careless with his fishing equipment."

Johnny, now back in the room again, sighed. "Oh, Ma. It was an accident. I'll try to be more careful."

"Just as a reminder, I told him he would pay for this visit out of his allowance."

"Your husband has good insurance," I pointed out. "I'm sure it'll pay the bill. No sutures were needed, and she's already up to date on her tetanus vaccination."

Johnny was heading for the main door to exit. Mrs. Morton frowned, placed her right index finger over her lips, and motioned me closer. "I want him to worry about it for a while, that's all."

Not wanting to interfere with parental discipline, I smiled and retained my unspoken thoughts about the incident. No doubt he'd been careless, but I didn't want to cause him any more trouble than he was already in with his mother.

Later that evening as I enjoyed the park with my family, I couldn't help but wonder how many of Johnny's fishing trips would land him in the office during the summer months. School had only just let out until the fall semester, and he already had a good start on wreaking havoc on family members.

***

Three weeks later, I arrived at my office a few minutes early following morning rounds at the hospital in Glen Falls. I steered into my usual parking spot behind the building while congratulating myself for being on time.

Inside, I found Donna in the lab with a patient seated where she normally drew morning blood work. I paid little attention until I heard a familiar voice protesting, "Wait a minute, that really hurts."

With a sinking feeling, I turned to see Johnny Morton slumped over in the chair with Donna sponging sweat from his forehead. "What's going on?"

"It's Johnny. He's got a large fishing lure with hooks embedded in his right hand. He asked me to try to get it out, but it's simply punctured too far into his palm. I had the exam rooms all full, except for your office, so I had him sit down here. I thought he was going to faint before I got him seated, but when he felt better, he asked if I could pull the hooks out."

Examining the injury, I saw that he had an artificial frog bait with treble hooks on the end in his palm. Not one but two of the barbs had pierced deep enough to be invisible. "How in the world did you do this?"

"It's a sad story. I was on the lake at 5:30 this morning in my secret fishing spot. On the second cast, this monster bass grabbed my frog lure and ran with it. It took fifteen minutes to get him reeled to the bank. I thought he was all played out, but I guessed wrong. That old fish gave a giant leap into the air, flipped my frog out of his mouth, and left me with what you see here in my poor hand. He swam off into deep water while I fell over on the bank writhing in pain. He ruined my perfect morning."

He wasn't the only one with a morning in shambles. "Johnny, as soon as we have exam room 1 free, Donna will put you in there."

"Can't you give me some of that medicine like you gave Tammy first? I want the hurting to stop."

"You won't hurt so much if you'll stop trying to work it out of your skin. You're only driving it in deeper. Besides, I'm only going to use plain lidocaine to numb it, and the anesthetic might wear off before I can get to you. Wait here while I get my metal snips. I'll cut the lure off so we can get to the wound better."

Now thoroughly horrified, Johnny nearly shouted, "No! You can't do that."

"I'll be very careful not to cause you any more pain while I cut the hooks off."

"No. You don't understand. That was a whopper bass. My frog lure had him for a while. I don't want to lose such a great bait."

"You can buy another one."

"No, it won't be the same thing. This is my lucky lure!"

Disgusted now, I stepped back. "Really? Do you mean good luck or bad?"

"I'm sorry, Doc. I don't mean to be smart. But you know when a fella has a big fish on the line, there's just something about it. I know this is a lucky lure. That is the biggest bass I ever hooked."

I shook my head. "I give up, Johnny. But this will take longer that way. The second set of treble hooks is dangling free. One wrong move on your part and you'll have two treble hooks stuck in your palm." Then taking in his anguished countenance, I sighed audibly. He really was a decent kid. "But I'll try to save your frog lure intact. Donna, get some tape and cover the treble hook barbs, the three on the back hook and the one still free that's in his hand. Then we'll do what we can do."

Johnny was now all smiles, if only for a moment. "Thanks. I'll come over and cut your grass free of charge next week to return this favor. This really means a lot to me."

I left to see the first patient, unable to keep from smiling as Johnny once again began complaining while Donna gently wrapped up the business end of the unattached barbs. "Be careful. It's really tender."

"I am being careful." Donna was starting to lose her patience. If you'll just sit still and stop talking, this will go a lot faster."

***

About an hour later, I finally had the hooks removed and Johnny was resting on the cart. Being a fisherman myself, I knew a little about Johnny's love for the sport, but I still didn't understand why that particular lure had to be spared. The bass wouldn't know the difference in an identical frog lure.

He sat up on the cart, and I retrieved the lure from my surgery tray, where I'd placed it for safe keeping. Donna began wrapping a bandage about the wound as I gave final instructions.

"This wound was deeper than the one you gave your sister. I had to put in three stitches to close it up. Please don't get your hand in lake or pond water while the stitches are in place."

Consternation replaced Johnny's smile. "How long will that be?"

"Seven to ten days, depending on how fast you heal."

Johnny looked down briefly, but as he looked back up at me, a cherubic smile replaced the look of chagrin. "I'll wear a glove when I fish until it's healed." Obviously noticing my look of disbelief, he hurried on to say, "Really, you can count on me being careful."

I couldn't help but smile. "That will be a welcome change."

After Johnny left the exam room, Donna looked at me with a frown. "Do you really think he'll keep the wound clean?"

"I doubt it, but time will tell."

Chapter 8:

In Sickness and in Crisis

Startled by a blinding flash of lightning accompanied by a deafening clap of thunder, I glanced up just in time to see the neighbor's large oak swaying in the wind, about one hundred yards out in the field, as one of its gigantic limbs crashed to the ground. Outside, the brief stillness gave way to a blinding deluge as the large picture window in the lab rattled and rivulets of rain poured down the glass, obscuring the employee parking lot and shrubbery.

I jumped up, attempting to see through the pounding rain. Wind gusts hurled ripped-off leaves and small branches past as I watched in consternation. It had only been two years since a tornado swept over that same field, just missing our office as it wreaked havoc and destruction on neighboring towns and farms.

A brief relenting of the cloudburst improved my vision enough to see that there were no funnel clouds in sight. Momentarily relieved, I ran to the cabinet over the sink and switched on the weather radio, listening as the robotic voice ludicrously advised that the chance of rain was 50 percent today.

Disgusted now, I switched off the radio as Donna and Christine hurried in to check on the weather. "No help there. A fifty percent chance of rain indeed."

They couldn't hear me over the roar of the pounding rainstorm. I cupped my hands and yelled, "The weatherman said a fifty percent chance of rain."

Christine, frightened but able to sense the ironic humor, laughed nervously.

As suddenly as it had come, the wind and rain dwindled to a light steady rain, then rays of sun broke through the distant clouds and brightened the far end of the long pasture.

Smiling, Donna pointed out the window. "Oh, look. A rainbow."

Christine, visibly relieved, turned to go back to the waiting room. "I'll let the patients know the lightning hit that old oak tree. They'll be relieved that it isn't worse. Everyone gets on edge when a bad storm hits, after the tornado we had."

Donna resumed preparing patients to be seen. "Wendy and Roger Pearson just arrived. I'll have them in a room for you in a minute. Wendy is the first afternoon patient, and several others are already here for the afternoon appointments."

I nodded. The brief break in the clouds and the rainbow had already disappeared as rain drummed on the roof in a much more sedate manner. The dismal gray of the afternoon matched the mood I was in after reading Wendy's barium enema radiology report for the second time.

Apple core lesion in the proximal sigmoid colon, highly suspicious for carcinoma. Recommend colonoscopy and workup as indicated.

Wendy Pearson, age thirty-eight years, was a gregarious woman with a bubbly personality, as well as an unalterable optimist and the mother of two charming children. Why did it have to be such a nice person? Only four weeks ago, I had seen her for a yearly wellness checkup. I had found no problems, but as I looked over her answers to our general questionnaire, I noted that she had checked *Constipation – recent onset.*

Constipation is such a common and usually benign complaint that I didn't think too much about it until we had discussed it further during the visit. I replayed scenes from that visit in my mind while waiting on Donna to finish checking Wendy in.

"Tell me about your constipation, Wendy," I'd said. "Do you mean to say that your bowel movements are hard, infrequent, or both?"

"It's probably nothing, but Roger wanted me to mention it."

"Roger is right. It's not usually a serious symptom in someone your age, but I need to evaluate what is going on."

"Okay. My bowel movements have become smaller and harder to get out. Sometimes I have to strain a lot. They are a little less frequent, every two or three days instead of daily as in the past. I'm embarrassed to talk about it. Do you need to know anything else?"

"Don't be embarrassed. It's simply a normal body function that's necessary for life in all of us. So, yes, I want to know more. Is there any blood or change in color? Have there been any dietary or activity changes on your part? Do you drink plenty of water and fluids every day? Do you take any fiber?"

Wendy had held up both hands, palms facing me, laughing softly. "Okay. Okay. I get the message. This is the third degree, so here goes."

During the conversation, I had learned that she had not changed her diet or activities. And no, she did not take fiber. Her stools were fairly firm, smaller in circumference, without blood that she could see, some occasional mucus noted, usually accompanied by painful cramping.

"Have you lost any weight?"

"Maybe two or three pounds. Nothing to speak of, I'm sure." Countenance brightening, she leaned forward in conspiratorial manner. "I needed to lose those two or three pounds anyway. I'm ten pounds heavier than when Roger and I were married fifteen years ago. Don't tell Roger how much I weigh." She had smiled beautifully and sat back laughing at her little joke.

Donna opened the lab door, indicated that Wendy was ready, and then hurried on to check in more patients for the afternoon schedule.

With a deep sigh, I got up and reluctantly made my way to exam room 2. Exam room 1 still smelled of vomit from a sick child that morning, and we had decided to skip it until a more thorough cleaning of the carpet could be accomplished.

Opening the door, I was confronted with Roger's tightly drawn face as he sat subconsciously drumming his fingers on the small writing desk. He gave me a brief worried nod as Wendy looked up from a health magazine she had been reading, smiled, stuck out her hand, and clasped mine in a firm handshake.

Doing my best to hide my feelings, I managed a weak smile. "Hello, Wendy, Roger. How are you folks doing today?"

Roger leaned forward, rested his elbows on his thighs, laced his fingers and thumbs together, and cleared his throat nervously. "I'm okay, Doc. How about Wendy's report? What can you tell us?"

Wendy looked up expectantly, beaming at me. "Yes. How about my report card? Did I pass my test?"

I hesitated. How many times must I be the messenger of frightening news? "Wendy, Roger, we need to do more tests."

Roger straightened in his chair and folded his arms across his chest, momentarily unable to say anything.

Seated on his right side, Wendy reached over and patted him on the knee, then took his hand in hers. "I didn't do so good, huh?"

"Well, it wasn't normal." I swallowed the lump in my throat. "There's a lesion constricting your colon at the upper sigmoid area, about fourteen inches above the anal canal. The radiologist was unable to make a diagnosis, but very correctly advised further testing."

Roger tightened his grip on Wendy's hand. "What's a lesion? What does that mean?"

Wendy turned to look at him. "It's an abnormality, darling. Doc doesn't know what it is yet." She turned to look back at me. "Isn't that correct?"

"Yes, but how did you know what a lesion meant?"

"Remember, you asked me about my family history last visit?"

I nodded.

"I didn't know much beyond my maternal grandparents, but I called my aunt in Boston, and learned that my paternal grandparents both died of colon cancer. I've been reading about it and how it's diagnosed since then."

Astounded, Roger turned to stare at her. "I wondered why you were spending so much time at the library. You were doing your own research, weren't you?"

"Yes, dear. It seems to me that if there's a battle to fight, it's best to know the enemy that one is up against."

I gently got back into the conversation. "Wendy, you then know that there can be both benign and malignant causes of a lesion. You have a partial blockage. You didn't feel like having a rectal exam the other day, but did you bring in the stool Hematest cards I sent home with you?"

"Oh yes. I almost forgot. I have them here in this plastic baggy. Will you check them now?"

"Certainly we will. Excuse me for a few minutes while I add the reagent to test for blood."

As I left the room, Roger still sat staring at Wendy in open-mouthed amazement.

Within a very short time, I had the answer and went back to discuss the findings and the next step with the Pearsons. They were sitting silently when I returned, hand in hand, and a tear trickled down Roger's left cheek.

I took a deep breath. "There is blood in both specimens according to the reagents. First of all, I want you to know that this could still be a benign lesion. Crohn's disease of the colon can cause constricting lesions, but it's not a cancerous condition. There are other non-cancerous lesions that can sometimes cause a similar appearance on X-ray."

Wendy's face remained calm and serene. "What's the next step? You said that my blood tests were all normal except for a mild anemia, hemoglobin of 11, I believe."

"That's correct and very important. There were no abnormal liver or renal function tests. It's likely that whatever the lesion is, it very well may be an isolated problem that has a good chance at cure. With your permission, I'd like you to see a surgeon in Glen Falls. I recommend Dr. Rob Hendrick. He has a great personality and wonderful bedside manner. I have utmost confidence in his ability. He has successfully cared for many of my patients."

"I've heard good things about him, but it'll be up to Wendy." Roger had regained some of his composure. "She has to make the call."

"I'll be glad to see him. I've already talked to several ladies in our neighborhood about him. He has a good reputation in the community."

I had to smile. "Give me a few minutes and I'll have your appointment. Dr. Hendrick is seeing patients in the office this afternoon. I'll call him now."

Within fifteen minutes, Donna was escorting the couple to checkout with Christine. They left hand in hand, Wendy continuing to put on a brave front for her very frightened husband.

***

After seeing the last patient, I prepared to go home. I turned the coffee pot off, dumped the stale coffee in the bottom of the carafe down the sink drain, and placed my stethoscope in my black bag. When I went to see if everything was secured for the night, Christine and Donna soberly confronted me.

Donna acted as spokesman. "We want to know what you think."

Although momentarily puzzled, the light suddenly dawned on me. "Oh, you mean about Wendy Pearson. Am I right?"

"Right," they responded in unison. These ladies weren't just healthcare workers. They truly became involved with the human drama and misery so often encountered in medical practice. They cared about our patients.

"We can hope for the best. Maybe the lesion is benign. But an apple core lesion is advanced enough to encircle an entire segment of the colon, choking off the normal passage of stool. The good news is that there is no sign of disease elsewhere as of now, at least by my limited blood testing and examination. If this is cancer, perhaps it is curable."

Donna shook her head. "We're just feeling sad about her and her family. Franklin is only ten. Francis is thirteen. If this is cancer, it's really sad. I think she knows and suspects it's cancer. She's just putting on a brave front for her family."

"I suppose you're right. I have to confess that I don't have a good feeling about it either." I glanced out the waiting room picture window facing the street. Sunlight illuminated the well-kept lawns across the road. Already, mists of water vapor were rising from the rapidly heating concrete streets and sidewalks. "Hopefully tomorrow will be a better day. The weather report is favorable at least. That is, if you can believe it."

The last comment evoked brief smiles from the ladies. Christine assumed her most authoritative robotic voice. "Yes, if you can believe it. Indeed!"

***

Two weeks later, Dr. Hendrick and I anxiously awaited the pathology report in the OR (operating room). I assisted him, retracting the wound as he sutured the distal and proximal colon together. He had excised the diseased segment with safe margins on either side and sent it to the hospital lab for analysis, along with several pelvic lymph nodes. Fredrick Howard, hospital pathologist, would very soon convey his findings.

Dr. Hendrick had already explored the abdomen manually and found no evidence of other disease, hence we were very hopeful. We already knew from a colonoscopy biopsy done by him that Wendy had a well-differentiated adenocarcinoma, likely slow growing and with a better prognosis, unlike a poorly differentiated cancer. As he put the finishing stitches in joining the segments together, the report of one positive regional pelvic lymph node came back.

Wendy had opted for an initial partial resection rather than more radical surgery, at least to begin with. She had been advised that more radical surgery might be needed at some point, but all preop testing had pointed to a possible surgical cure. Dr. Gerald Stanberry, oncologist from Indianapolis, made biweekly rounds in our county hospital. His extensive testing had disclosed no sign of metastasis or spread of the cancer. But here it was, cancer in one out of fifteen pelvic nodes.

Disappointed, Dr. Hendrick completed the operation, finally placing Steri-Strips for skin closure. He removed his mask, gown, and gloves. "Carl, we might as well go tell the family what we've found. I know they're anxiously waiting for some answers. I sure wish all the lymph nodes had been clear. Still, with help from oncology, she may be all right."

We rode the elevator down from the third floor and made our way to the main waiting room near the front entrance of the hospital. When Roger Pearson saw us coming, he leaped from the leather chair and hurried to meet us. He was followed by their children. Older relatives came to stand with them. The children stood one on each side of their dad while he rested his arms around their shoulders.

Dr. Hendrick waited until the entire family was in position to hear the results. Then he began his description of the main points of the surgery. "First of all, she did very well during anesthesia and surgery. She is in post-op recovery, where she'll be for about an hour or so. When she's stable, she'll be moved to a room on the third floor where the surgical patients are cared for. She won't be in ICU unless she develops some other complication, which at this time I don't anticipate. Second, I believe we got all of the colon cancer resected from the colon itself, and anastomosed or hooked the segments back together again."

He then hesitated for a moment. "Third, unfortunately, she had one positive node identified among many tested, meaning that there was a small regional spread of the carcinoma. The lymph nodes are protective filters against infections and tumors. Perhaps the lymph node contained the disease. She may not have any more problems, but we can't know that for sure now. When she's recovered from surgery, Dr. Stanberry, the oncologist she consulted with pre-operatively, will direct future treatment and care."

Suddenly, everyone was talking at once until Roger raised his hand for silence. "Sorry for the outburst. I guess you both know that we're all very anxious. Speaking for my family, we want to thank you for what you've already done to help Wendy. And we would like to know if she needs radiation and some other treatments."

Dr. Hendrick nodded to me, indicating that he left further discussion up to me. He waited with me as I answered the best I could. "It's likely that both radiation and chemotherapy will be necessary. As you know, there are a lot of side effects with either option, but Dr. Stanberry will be able to guide you through the process. And we'll be there to help when needed. Our goal is that she has the best care possible and state-of-the-art treatment for the colon cancer. As I said before, I'm very hopeful because the cancer is well differentiated, meaning highly organized as a tissue, as opposed to poorly organized. The type she has is normally slow to grow, slow to spread, and more responsive to therapy if it does spread. I believe she's had this for several months now for it to have formed a constrictive ring around the sigmoid colon, only causing symptoms the last few weeks."

Roger shook hands with each of us. "Thanks again, both of you. I'm sure I'll have more questions later. Just now I feel a little overwhelmed and frightened. I hope you'll bear with me as we go through this with Wendy."

"We'll be there for both you and Wendy," I assured him.

Dr. Hendrick added, "We certainly will."

Chapter 9:

Falling Shadows

A year passed, during which time it became obvious that Wendy Pearson was losing her battle with cancer. In conjunction with the oncologist, I had been meeting her in the ER at our county hospital to give the orders and be present for the administration of 5-Fluorouricil (5FU) so she wouldn't have to make the long trip to Indianapolis every time she started a new cycle of chemotherapy. This was handled on an outpatient basis for her convenience.

With the other chemotherapeutic agents and radiation treatments she had undergone, Wendy had lost most of her hair and developed extreme fatigue and anorexia. Her weight declined steadily until she weighed only eighty-seven pounds.

One day in late fall, I met Wendy and Roger in the ER as usual. She was to start another cycle of 5FU, to be given while I made rounds in the hospital. I entered the exam room where she and Roger waited, but stopped transfixed in the doorway, shocked at Wendy's appearance.

Previously, even on her worst days, Wendy had made it a point to look her best. She always greeted the staff with at least a wan smile. Despite our best efforts, cancer had spread to the lungs and liver by now, defying all our efforts at treatment. Her physical appearance revealed in stark reality what the ravages of metastatic carcinoma was doing to her internally.

Forcing myself to enter, I proceeded to the side of the cart, stopping to place my hand on Roger's shoulder while I talked with Wendy. She lay curled up in the fetal position with a pale complexion, a face and body skeletal in appearance, and a scalp covered with a yellow scarf formed into a turban that was tied in a knot at the back of her head. The only sound she made was an intermittent soft moaning.

"Hello, Wendy."

She opened her eyes to gaze dully up at me. "Hi. I'm not feeling so well this morning."

We were interrupted by one of the ER nurses entering to hand me Wendy's CBC, just completed in the lab.

I read the results in silence. Hemoglobin 7.3, hematocrit 21, WBC 1000, platelets 20,000.

"Your blood count is quite low this morning. I don't think we will be giving you the medication. Your white blood count has dropped to levels that make you a high risk to develop an infection if we proceed as planned. Unfortunately, due to low platelets you could have bleeding complications if we continue today."

Roger stifled a sob. "That's what we want to talk to you about." He paused for several seconds. "We've been talking recently about ..." He shuddered as soft sobbing prevented him from completing his thoughts.

Wendy feebly reached for his hand, looked up at me, and smiled. "What Roger means to say is that I've decided to stop all cancer treatment except for comfort measures."

I became choked up at that point.

Noticing it, Wendy next reached for my hand. "It's all right, Doc. I can't go on being this sick and helpless. My greatest sorrow is having to leave my family, but I know I'm at the end of my resources."

No one spoke for a full minute as I processed her speech. "Is there anything I can do to make you more comfortable now?"

"Perhaps you could keep me in the hospital. I know my time is short. I'd just like to be a little more comfortable."

"No problem. I'll make the arrangements right now. Is there anything else I can do?"[2]

Wendy hesitated, then nodded for Roger to explain. "Wendy and I have been doing a lot of thinking. We consider ourselves good people, but we've seldom attended church or prayed, although we do believe in God and that Jesus is His Son. In the past few months, we've been reading the Bible together as a family, but we don't have a pastor, and, well, both Wendy and I feel the need to talk to a minister. I guess we just need to know that we're ready for heaven when the time comes. The fact is we're both afraid of dying. We know that you're a Christian and thought maybe you could have your minister counsel and pray with us."

That was the least I could do. "I'll be glad to have my pastor call on you. I'll contact him this morning."

"Thanks. Wendy and I really appreciate all you've done for her."

"I only wish I could do more."

***

Over the next week and a half, I cared for Wendy as she deteriorated physically, slowly losing her hold on life. I kept her as comfortable as I could, and her children and extended family were allowed extra latitude in visiting in her room.

My minister did call on the Pearsons the very day I had asked him, and he continued to visit and pray with them every day until the end. Roger took a leave of absence from work to be at her bedside. As Wendy sweetly and peacefully faded into the land of lengthening

---

[2] In the 1970s, hospice was in its infancy in the United States and not available in our area. In addition, hospital admissions for terminal cancer care were quite common.

shadows, she became an inspiration to all who cared for her during that time.

Following prayer that first day after admission to the hospital, during a pastoral visit she had received assurance that she was forgiven and ready to meet God. Her family followed her example in prayer and confession, so on the day of her death, there was a bittersweet sense of her departing this life into a better and eternal one where she would await being reunited with her family some glorious day. She had spent her last days very graciously, thanking her caretakers profusely, talking with and spending quiet times with her family, and praising and thanking her Lord for faith and courage in the midst of profound suffering.

***

Roger eventually remarried after meeting Elsa, a widow from church with a six-year-old son to raise. The new family unit also continued to honor me by allowing me to care for them over the next several years.

As I drove through the countryside one sunny afternoon about two years later, I noticed Roger and Elsa with the three children decorating graves in the little cemetery outside Glen Oaks. I guided my car through the gate, stopping to say hello.

It was gratifying to note that they had decorated the gravesites of both Wendy and Matthew, Elsa's first husband. I don't always know why and how things happen to good people, but I'm glad there can still be happy endings after long periods of living in the darkness and shadows of this life.

Chapter 10:

More Fishermen's Tales

L abor Day would arrive next Monday, and my family was visiting relatives in southern Indiana. I planned to leave Glen Oaks and drive south seventy miles to join them after office hours on Saturday morning. We were to spend the weekend celebrating the holiday and return home Monday afternoon. Another physician would make rounds and take my calls until Monday evening. I rarely afforded myself such latitude, but I felt exhausted emotionally and physically.

My family had departed Wednesday morning for an early start to the holiday, leaving me to fend for myself for a few days. Hence, I arrived early in Glen Oaks and stopped at the general store and pharmacy owned by my friend, Barry House, the town pharmacist.

He and his wife, Ethel, sold everything from blue jeans to small farm implements, fencing wire, animal feed, tools, nails, wood screws, fishing gear, and live bait. You name it, they had it.

At the back of the store, Barry spent most of his day in the confines of the pharmacy filling prescriptions, while Ethel and her daughters ran a soda fountain and small restaurant up front, complete with old-fashioned booths for those who preferred them, barstools for others. Two of their older boys waited on customers and rang up general merchandise sales. It was a country store with personality plus.

The screen door protested with a loud screeching sound as I entered, then slammed shut with a bang, powered by the tightly loaded spring mechanism. A small bell over the door further announced my entrance, though with all the noise from the door opening, I'm not sure why the bell was needed.

Ethel looked up from the counter where she had been chatting with one of the customers. "Morning, Doc. How are you this fine day?" Not pausing for me to answer, she continued, "Wife and kids must be out of town. What'll you have for breakfast?"

"What's the special this morning?"

"Ham and eggs. Milk and toast with all the hot coffee you can drink. All for two fifty. You can't beat it anywhere in town." She grinned, curtsied, and then indicated that I should take a seat.

She was so right. It was the only breakfast restaurant in Glen Oaks. But she and her daughters were wonderful cooks. I preferred eating there to the breakfast establishments in the larger city of Glen Falls, where the county hospital was located.

Farmers get up early, so the Glen Oaks Pharmacy, General Store, and Restaurant opened for business at 5:30 a.m. Monday through Saturday, closing at 8:00 p.m. daily. It was closed all day on Sunday. I had purposely made rounds early so I could eat leisurely before office hours, then spend time savoring my steaming hot coffee while reading the *Glen Oaks Bulletin*, published biweekly on Tuesdays and Thursdays.

The newspaper mainly highlighted local town events and happenings: the latest births and deaths, marriages and engagements, town hall meeting schedules with summaries of the latest issues and votes, the Glen Oaks High School football or basketball scores and stats depending on the season, and humorous stories about friends and neighbors, all in good fun.

I had just started reading the preseason Glen Oaks High football stats when a voice beside me interrupted my concentration. "Mind if I join you?"

Glancing up, I looked into the beaming face of Johnny Morton. "Not at all. Have a seat. I was just reading about your latest exploits on the football field in this morning's *Bulletin*."

He slid into the seat across from me in the booth, a pleased look on his face. "Aw, Doc. That stuff is okay, but it won't get a fella far in life."

I gave him a quizzical look. "You're being too modest. It says right here that you're starting quarterback and team captain for your senior year. It also predicts that you'll easily be the most valuable player for the team."

"Yeah, well. That's all okay, but my goal is not professional football. Not many guys ever get into the pros."

"No, but maybe you'll get a football scholarship for college. That could mean a lot for your family and for you."

"Who needs college? That's what I wanted to talk to you about. I've definitely decided on a career. I wanted you to be the first to know."

"Really? Why me?"

"Because I may need your services from time to time."

Oh, boy. "What in the world are you going to do with your life that you'll need my help?"

"I've definitely made up my mind to be a professional fisherman. You contributed to my decision, you know."

Concerned by this announcement, I felt the need to intervene. "Do you know how difficult it would be to be a professional fisherman and make a decent living?"

"Not really. But I'll do it. I just know I will."

"Why are you attributing this decision to me? I hope you haven't told your folks that I'm advising you in this matter."

"Naw. Nothin' like that. My folks don't know about this from nothin'."

"You mean you haven't told them yet?"

"Exactly. I won't tell them I got the idea in your office."

I was becoming upset and spoke a little harshly, I'm afraid. "That's not possible."

"Sure it is. I've read every page of *Sports Afield* and *Field and Stream* that you have in the office, especially the stories by their fishing editors. Man, that'll be the life. Fishing all day and writing about it at night, traveling to fishing tournaments and getting to fish all the big lakes in the country."

I was truly astounded now. "You weren't in the office long enough to read all of those monthly magazines. How can you have any idea what you're getting into?"

"Christine, Doc."

"What do you mean, 'Christine'?"

"She let me take them home overnight. I always brought them back the next morning."

Great. "Sorry, I didn't realize I was running a lending library."

"Now don't get sore. I'm sure to bring you a lot of business. You know how I tangle with fishing lures. I'll bring you all my business."

I folded my newspaper and laid it down, unable to think of an appropriate response.

Johnny just smiled, turned, and called out to Ethel, "How about a chocolate soda, Mrs. House?"

Ethel shook her head. "We don't make them this early, Johnny."

"But I'm celebrating this morning."

"I don't care what you're doing or why. The soda fountain isn't open yet."

Sherry, the Houses' oldest daughter and a sophomore at Glen Oaks High, hurried to our booth, obviously overcome with hero worship and perhaps puppy love. "Johnny, if you come back at noon today, I'll be glad to fix you a chocolate soda, on the house so to speak. I read all about you being the captain of the football team this year. It's a great thing to celebrate."

Momentarily puzzled, Johnny could only stare at her. "Celebrate that? Not hardly. I'm celebrating because I'm going to be a professional fisherman. Now that's something to have a party over."

I interrupted the lively discourse. "I'm sorry to have to leave such erudite company, but it's time for me to go to work. You two have a wonderful day." I stood, then directed one last comment to Johnny. "Are you going fishing this weekend?"

"I sure am. But I'm not waiting for Saturday. Starting today, I'm fishing all day every day through Labor Day. But don't tell Ma. She won't like it a bit. I suppose I'll take time out to go to Sunday school, at least."

I assumed a sarcastic tone of voice. "That's very thoughtful of you, Johnny. I really just wanted to know when you would need my services next. I'll be prepared for later today."

"Aw, Doc. Don't be funnin' me. This is serious."

"It certainly is," I responded. "Be sure you don't get a hook in your eye. I can't fix that."

Sherry scooted in where I had been seated. "Johnny, please tell me all about it. You lead such an exciting life."

A surprised look crossed Johnny's face. "Yeah, sure. I didn't know girls were so interested in fishing."

She beamed in open admiration. "Well, I certainly am. Please tell me about the fish you've caught."

A little uncertain of himself now, Johnny began telling Sherry of his fishing exploits.

Ethel stood behind the counter, hands on her hips and a look of exasperation on her face. "I lose more helpers that way. Couldn't you stop them?"

As I paid my bill on the way out, I commented, "It looks to me like the fisherman is now the big fish being played on a line, and just like an ignorant fish, he has no idea of the nature of the bait dangled before him."

Ethel laughed loudly. "You are so right. He's a hapless victim and doesn't know it."

***

Tuesday morning after Labor Day dawned with a cool

westerly breeze and forty-seven degrees on the outdoor office thermometer, a harbinger of an early fall. I hadn't heard anything from Johnny during office hours last Thursday, Friday, or Saturday, and had given him little thought. That would soon change.

Halfway through the morning, I heard a disturbance in the waiting room. I was between patients, and paused near the entrance to the patient hallway, catching the excited conversation.

"Wow, where did you catch that whopper?"

"It's a secret. Can't tell you where my fishin' hole is."

I immediately knew the source of the enthusiastic conversation. In the waiting room, I encountered a group of men clustered around Johnny in a football-like huddle.

Johnny noticed me right away. "Doc, come look at my fish." He held up a monstrous channel catfish on a stringer, dripping a stream of water on the carpet as it flipped about in protest. Seeing my displeasure, Johnny looked down at the growing wet spot on the tan carpet. "Sorry. Didn't mean to get the floor all wet."

"Would you mind taking that back outdoors?"

"Sure. Sure. Sorry."

He started for the door, followed by four of his admirers, when another thought interrupted my peace of mind. "Say, Johnny, aren't you supposed to be in school? I distinctly heard the school bus stop outside to pick up students this morning. First day of school for the fall semester, isn't it?"

Johnny paused with his hand on the exit doorway. "About that. Well, I fished all night." Noticing my frown, he quickly continued, "The catfish were really biting. I have a stringer of four more big ones outside. I threw the smaller ones back in to grow some more. Time kind of got away from me."

At that moment, a wrathful Mrs. Morton opened the door. "Jonathan Morton, get that fish out of Doc's office this instant. I told you to have him look at your right hand and forearm, not that silly fish. Now go throw that in the back of the pickup with the rest of the fish and get back in here at once."

There were few secrets in a small town. Mrs. Morton vented to the entire waiting room. "I just found out that Johnny was out all night fishing. I opened his door to get him up for school at 6:00 a.m., and low and behold, he wasn't there. He just came bouncing in a little while ago asking if breakfast was ready." Shaking her head in disgust, she stepped to Christine's window to check her wayward son in for a visit.

Within a short time, Donna had Johnny seated in the lab as his mother hovered nearby. I continued to see scheduled patients while she evaluated his wounds. "I want to have a look at your right hand an arm, so you'll have to take your jacket off and roll up your sleeve."

Johnny reluctantly complied with her request.

Shocked by what she saw, Donna stared. "You'll have to take your shirt off so I can see this better."

"Oh, all right." Johnny carefully peeled his shirt off, careful not to injure his arm any further.

"How and when did this happen?"

Mrs. Morton sucked in her breath and turned away at the sight of his right upper extremity. Multiple abrasions that he had so artfully hidden were now in full view. The back of his hand and palm had multiple superficial lineal abrasions, some with dried blood still present, several still oozing serous fluid contaminated with dirt and developing a honey-like crusting in several wound areas. His hand had developed an intense erythematous rash with intense red streaks extending from his forearm to his upper arm, ending about six inches below his shoulder.

"Probably about eleven last night. That's when I landed that biggest fish. He had swallowed my artificial crank bait. Did you know that catfish will bite on them too? And I wasn't about to lose it."

Donna looked at her watch. "Almost twelve hours ago. What did you do to retrieve it?"

"I did what any fisherman worth his salt would do. I reached way down in his mouth while he chewed on my hand, and finally got it back. I snagged myself with the hook barbs a couple of times, but most of the scratches came from him chewing on my hand."

Mrs. Morton had pulled out one of our chairs to sit down. The color that had drained away from her face slowly returned. "Why in the world did you do that? Couldn't you just get it back when you cleaned him later?"

"No. Ma, you don't know much about fishing. That lure was the only one of its kind that I had with me. I wanted to catch another big catfish and had to have that lure."

Donna managed a grim smile. "Did you catch any more with that same lure?"

Johnny dropped his head and hesitated. "No, I guess I didn't."

Exasperated now, Mrs. Morton asked, "Johnny, when will you ever learn?"

"Aw, Ma. Can't you give a fella a break?"

Donna prepared a basin of soapy water to cleanse the wounds and set it aside. "I need to check your temperature. Your face is really flushed."

Johnny sighed. "I don't feel so good either."

While he held the thermometer in his mouth, she opened a fresh surgical sponge brush to clean the wounds. She then retrieved the thermometer after an appropriate interval and held it up before her eyes. "Your temp is 103.2. I'm afraid you have a bad infection in your arm. Doc will need to look at this after I clean it up. You'll probably have to go to the hospital for treatment."

Now fully alarmed, Johnny stared wide-eyed at Donna. "You can't be serious. Can't you just give me a shot of penicillin? It always does me a lot of good."

"Doc will decide what to give you, but I think this calls for more than a penicillin shot."

Donna summoned me between patients and gave a brief report, and I entered the lab to inspect Johnny's wounds. Startled by the angry, inflamed wounds on the back of his right hand and forearm, I picked up his wrist to flex and rotate the forearm for a better look at the other side.

Johnny winced. "Careful, Doc. It's really sore."

"Sorry. I'm trying to be careful. How did you stand this all night long?"

"I guess I had a lot of adrenaline pumping, like you explained to me once before about my heart beating faster after running cross-country. I didn't notice the pain until I got quiet here in the office." He looked down at his wounds. "In fact, I'm feeling faint."

Donna grabbed the smelling salts from the cabinet above the sink and soon had him revived. She then proceeded to gently sponge and clean the wounds.

"Does this really mean the hospital?" he asked.

"I'm afraid so. This is not something to treat at home. According to our records, you're up to date on your tetanus vaccine."

Johnny smiled in relief.

"However, with an infected wound of this degree in such a short time, we'll need to give you a protective shot of tetanus immune globulin."

He sighed. "Really, Doc? This just isn't my day."

***

Johnny Morton spent a miserable week in the hospital on IV cephalexin and tetracycline to cover for freshwater bacterial infection. With his basic healthy constitution, he soon improved and was ready for discharge home.

After reviewing his chart that morning, I entered his room. "How are you feeling today?"

"I'm feeling great and ready to go home. How about it, Doc?"

"Let's have one more look at that arm." I inspected his arm and found no more redness or swelling. The swollen, tender lymph nodes in his right axilla (armpit) had gone back to normal, and the red streaks of lymphangitis and the diffuse redness and swelling of cellulitis had resolved. I put his arm and shoulder through a passive range of motion, checking for any soreness or impairment. Finally, I had him actively move his arm through a complete range of motion and noted that he manifested no evidence of soreness or pain.

He stared at me with growing impatience as I again took my chair at his bedside, shaking my head and frowning.

"I don't get it. I feel fine. Why can't I go home?"

I could no longer restrain my mirth and began chuckling out loud. "I was just having a little fun with you. I never said you couldn't go home. I believe you're more than ready for release this morning."

Relief flooded his face. "You had me worried for a minute."

He stuck out his now-healed right hand. "Thanks. Thanks for everything. And you know what? Maybe I won't be a professional fisherman. I'm still proud of my catch, but I don't want to go through this again."

"So, then, are you thinking about college and another career?"

"Yeah, thanks to you. I enjoyed watching you and your staff care for me. That is, after I thought about it later. Maybe I'll be an EMT or a paramedic. I'd like that a lot."

"Well, you have plenty of time to decide as you finish your schooling. I really would prefer you arriving in the office to help with patients, and not to show off your catch of the day."

Johnny smiled, and we had a good laugh together.

Chapter 11:

To Live Again

"**D**oc, there's nothing you can do about it. I'll find a way to die. I've nothin' to live for any longer." Charley McNair sat on the side of the hospital bed in a darkened private room with the curtains drawn closed. His head hung down as he hoarsely spoke the slow, slightly slurred words.

"Charley, there's no need for that."

He was already shaking his head. "I don't want to go on. I'm tired of fightin'."

Charley had been diagnosed with hypothyroidism twenty years ago at age forty-five. This morning he had been admitted by the ER doctor, Jerome Hayden, a couple of hours before I arrived at the hospital to start rounds at 7:00 a.m.

Jerry's strident voice had awakened me before my alarm went off. "Jerome here. I've got your patient Charley McNair in the ER. I can't send him home and the shrinks won't take him in Indy until he's stabilized. He intentionally quit taking his Synthroid months ago. Now he's in trouble, not quite myxedema coma, but on the way. He's a nutcase, not too bright. He thought stopping his thyroid meds would be a quick way to die."

I decided to see Charley first thing on arriving at the hospital. None of my patients were in labor. Nothing else was as pressing. Now I sat at the bedside trying to reason with him while Buddy Crawford, Charley's good friend and bass-fishing buddy, sat in the far corner of the room, a worried expression on his face.

Charley refused to make eye contact with either of us.

After another uncomfortable silence, I leaned forward and gently placed my hand on Charley's knee. "Why do you want to die? You still haven't told me. You have a good wife and a family that loves you. I don't understand."

Charley just stared at the floor, shaking his head, refusing to respond further.

Exasperated, I turned to Buddy. "Do you know what's going on with our friend Charley?"

"Doc, he's been severely depressed ever since our foreman told him he had to retire when he reached sixty-five. That was six months ago. The company has new owners and new rules. His birthday is next week. Sara had me come and get his guns last week until Bob, their son, could get here from Oklahoma and take charge of them. I've done everything I know to do, but Charley won't listen to me anymore."

I turned my attention back to Charley. "I really need you to answer my questions. You know that I've always tried to help you. Right?"

Charley finally nodded, acknowledging that at least he had heard me. A hopeful sign. After another prolonged silence, he looked up. "What do you want to know?"

"When did you stop taking your thyroid medication?"

"I don't know. Several months ago."

"Did Sara know?"

Charley hung his head again. "She thinks she knows everything about me. Not hardly. Not till two or three weeks ago. She found my pill bottle still full from last winter."

"Filled five or six months ago?"

"Yeah. About."

"Did you plan to stop your medicine in hope of dying?"

Charley only nodded.

"What about your guns? Why did Sara take them?"

Charley merely shrugged again. Another prolonged silence.

Visibly agitated, Buddy interrupted. "Doc, if Charley will allow me, I'll tell you what happened."

Charley mumbled, "Do whatever you want. I don't care anymore."

"Sara found him sitting on a chair in the garage with a loaded revolver, spinning the chamber, just staring at the wall. She thought he was about to use it on himself and screamed. She ran to him and held out her hand, and he surrendered the gun, but not until he held it in his palm for a while. You can see why we're so worried."

This information really concerned me. "Would you really have shot yourself, Charley?"

"Don't know. Maybe."

"What stopped you?"

"I didn't want her to see me blowin' my brains out."

With a story that troubling, it was several seconds before I could continue my line of questioning. "What about your medicine?"

"I thought I might die, like I already told you."

"Were you seriously thinking that would be a good way to kill yourself?"

"Sure. I don't know nothin' about medicine. I thought it would work."

"When you realized it would be a very slow way to die, you thought about hurrying up the process?"

"Yeah. I guess."

"But why, Charley?"

Belligerent now, he groused, "You're a smart man. You tell me."

At least I had him angry. That could be a start back to the land of the living. "I think you're a selfish, mean-spirited old man."

Charley clenched his fists, face flushed and eyes glaring at me. "You can't talk to me like that."

"Yeah? Well, why not? You only think of yourself. So you want to die. You don't care about Sara or your son, Bob. You don't even care how it affects Buddy, a lifelong friend of yours. It doesn't matter what they think or how they'll cope with your death. Just so you get what you want. Am I right or not?"

Charley looked like he had been punched in the gut and had all the air sucked out of him. Ever so slowly, he relaxed his clenched fists, glanced to his right at Buddy, reached for his woolen house coat lying at the foot of the bed, ponderously pushed himself up, and slowly began to pace back and forth by the bedside as I moved out of his way.

For a couple of minutes, the only sound came from Charley pacing, finally making his way to the window on the other side of his bed, the one that looked out on the green park-like lawn of the hospital where stately oaks graced the landscape. Head bowed, hands clasped behind his back, facing away from me, he stood like a statue for some time.

Finally, Charley broke the silence. "Know what, Doc? You're absolutely right. I was mad when you first told me about myself, but I gotta hand it to you. You hit the nail right smack on the head. For months now, ever since they told me I was through at work, I've not thought about anyone but poor me. Not thinkin' about Sara, or Bob, or my friend Buddy. Just about me. I guess I'm a low-down skunk. Don't know why either one of you are even putting up with me now."

I carefully made my way to his side, and we both stood gazing out the window for some time. Trying not to let on that I noticed a tear trickling slowly down his cheek, I broke the silence. "Charley, it's a big, wide world outside that window. There's always hope for the man who doesn't give up. And you know something else? I really don't think you're a mean old man. You're a caring person. I just wanted to wake you up to that reality again. I still count you as a friend and a good neighbor."

In a voice made doubly husky by lack of his medication and the effort to choke back sobs, Charley turned and took my hand, blinking his eyes, and said, "Thanks. Thanks for caring about an old fool like me."

As I bid the two men a good day, I looked back on a beautiful scene. Buddy had his arms wrapped about his lifelong friend and fishing partner, squeezing him in a giant bear hug as both men shed a few tears together.

At the nurses station, Ann Kilgore supervised the day shift that morning. "Good morning, Doc. What about Charley? Do we need suicide precautions?"

I thought a minute, then glanced down the hall and saw

Charley and Buddy out of the room, walking and talking together. I motioned toward them before replying. "I don't think it'll be necessary now. Charley has a new outlook on living."

Ann walked around the counter and stood with hands on her hips, staring at the two men. "I believe you're right. That's great."

After ordering the Synthroid to be started at an initially lower dose due to his condition, I decided to go by the ER and see if Jerome Hayden was still on duty. I wanted to tell him that his "nutcase" was okay.

Chapter 12:

When Life Hangs in the Balance

"Ⅰf you refuse a blood transfusion, you and your baby both may die."

Panting and groaning with another hard contraction, Sue Harvey shrieked at me, "I won't take blood! You know it's against my religion!"

"I know, Sue, but I had to be sure. Where's Loren? I need to let him know and be sure we're all on the same page, just in case."

The contraction eased off and Sue calmed a little. "He's on his way from work. And we're on the same page. We've been of the Jehovah's Witness persuasion for a long time. When you took my case, you promised."

"I know. Believe me, I know. And I'll honor my promises. But I still need to talk with Loren as soon as possible. Meanwhile, I've already called in the surgery crew and am waiting on Dr. Hendrick to call me back. He's the general surgeon I mentioned to you a few minutes ago."

Mildred Long, the evening OB charge nurse, poked her head into the labor room just as another strong contraction started. "Dr. Matlock, I have Dr. Hendrick on the phone. I'll be able to stay with her now. I had to call in extra help for labor and delivery since I only have one aide tonight."

I glanced at Sue, who gripped the side rails with both hands and pulled her legs up as she stifled another scream. Then hurrying to the nearby small desk in the hallway, I grabbed the black phone from its cradle and pushed the flashing light indicating call waiting on line

2. "Dr. Hendrick?"

"Carl, you sound excited. What's up?"

"Rob, thank goodness you called back quickly. I have a twenty-eight-year-old gravida four, para three mother in labor with a baby in fetal distress. When her membranes ruptured, I put on a fetal scalp monitor an hour ago. For the last ten minutes, the baby has been experiencing distress with an early deceleration pattern on the monitor. She is only dilated five centimeters, and there's moderate bleeding."

"Get everybody there. I'll be right in. Call in the surgery crew. See if Bill Johnson can help us with anesthesia." He started to hang up.

"Wait. I need to tell you the family is Jehovah's Witness. She is consenting to surgery but refusing blood. Her hematocrit is only 27 with a hemoglobin of 9.0 prior to moderate bleeding."

A brief pause ensued on the other end of the line. Finally Rob answered, "Well, it can't be helped. We'll do what we can. Be sure the appropriate family members are informed. Get whatever you can in writing. See you soon."

Sharon Cunningham, OB nursing assistant, tapped me on the shoulder as I hung up the phone. "Mr. Harvey is here. I told him to wait by the nursing desk out front."

"Thanks, Sharon. Could you get Dr. Johnson on the phone while I talk with Mr. Harvey?"

"Sure thing."

I hurried down the hallway from labor and delivery to the OB nursing desk on the other side of the doorway.

Loren Harvey, at six feet five inches, towered five inches above me, jaw clenched, long face pinched, body rigid. "I hear something's wrong. Give it to me straight. I want to know the truth."

I stuck out my hand, but he either didn't see it or ignored it. "Loren, I'm sorry to have to tell you this, but your wife has an acute emergency. She is having some bleeding, more than I would normally expect. She's in hard labor with contractions about two minutes apart, and the baby is showing signs of serious distress."

"What do you mean by distress?"

"The baby has what we call an early deceleration pattern of

the heart rate."

Stunned now, Loren paled as his body slumped. "Is that very serious? I mean, is the baby going to die?"

I pointed to a couple of chairs that Sharon had just wheeled out from behind the OB station desk. "Let's sit down for a minute while I explain." I took him by the arm and helped him to a chair. All the color had drained from his face. Loren sat with his head bowed, wringing his hands, while I explained the situation. "I have to begin by telling you what I just told Sue. In a worst-case scenario, without a blood transfusion, she and the baby could both die."

He simply sat shaking his head. "Can't do that, Doc. You promised. We came to you because you are a man of faith. You don't believe like us, but you know what it is to have strong convictions. We're trusting you to honor your word."

"And I will honor my word to you. I just had to be sure you and your wife both agreed. You know there is another life at stake here."

Loren nodded. "I know. Please go on. What does it all mean, and what has to be done?"

"The heart rate of a baby normally decreases during a contraction as it peaks. That's normal. Then it speeds back up to a normal rate of 120 or so. What isn't normal is for the heartbeat to slow right away before a contraction really gets started. The baby's heartbeat is slowing into the low forties and staying down for a while after the contraction peaks and ends."

"That's bad, huh?"

"Yes, that's a bad sign. I've taken the liberty to call in Dr. Hendrick. He's a general surgeon who spent several years on a mission field doing all kinds of surgeries, including Caesarean sections. If your wife and baby survive whatever the problem is, we have to go to surgery as soon as everyone gets here for the procedure. Do you understand?"

Some of the color had returned to his face. "Yeah, I get it. Can I see Sue briefly?"

"Sure, come with me. I'll take you back. You can sit with her while everything is being readied for surgery."

As we entered the labor room, Sue was relaxing after a

particularly hard contraction. Sweat beaded her brow and flushed face. She had her head turned to the left, watching the monitor of the fetal heart recording. The heartbeat bottomed out at 42 before slowly returning to a regular 139.

"Look who's here, Sue. I believe you're acquainted with this young fella."

Loren took the chair that Mildred pushed in his direction. "Sit here on the other side of your wife. I'll be working on this side and need you out of the way." No one argued with her. She had just started the intravenous liter of normal saline that I had ordered and had other tasks to be rapidly completed. She rechecked Sue's BP and pulse, then nodded reassuringly. "BP 90/55. Pulse 105 but steady."

Sharon brought in the surgery consent forms for both to sign.

I went over them with the couple the best I could in a hurried manner. "This is a general consent form to do whatever is necessary during the procedure." I paused. "I'll strike out the sentence about receiving blood products. I'll initial that part and request that you both do the same to indicate your decision. Last of all, you'll sign here at the bottom. Okay?"

I had to try one more time. Sue was so pale and still bleeding. "I respect your personal beliefs, but I do have a question. The Bible was written mainly by ancient Hebrew writers. Jewish people today by a vast majority agree with blood transfusions to save lives. They don't interpret the Bible the way you do. The Bible prohibits eating blood, not receiving life-saving intravenous infusions of donated human blood. Have you ever thought about that?"

Loren glanced at Sue and nodded. "We've thought about it. We're not Jewish. No disrespect intended for the ancient writers, the Jewish people, or you."

"Okay. No offense intended on my part either. I'm just worried about Sue and the baby."

"We know. Believe me, we appreciate your concern. We just have to stick by our beliefs."

Fully resigned, I breathed a prayer for this young couple and was relieved to hear the surgery crew wheeling a cart in the hall outside the labor room.

Candice Benton, surgery charge nurse who also functioned as

chief scrub nurse when necessary, gave rapid-fire orders as Sue was transferred to her care. Turning to include me, she continued, "Dr. Matlock, you'd better hurry. Everyone else has changed and Dr. Hendrick is scrubbing in. All we need is the patient and you in the OR."

Within minutes I had donned a scrub suit, scrub hat, and mask. I completed the necessary scrubbing technique and entered the first surgical suite in the OR. Candice held out the sterile gloves one at a time and helped me get them on using sterile technique. She had already helped me into a sterile surgical gown, and I was soon ready.

Bill Johnson had started the anesthesia using a mild general anesthetic with Sue intubated and on a ventilator. The fetal heart monitor beat an ominous 35 beats per minute, resounding loudly in the hush of the OR. Sue's BP and pulse remained about the same, but when an OB patient finally crashes in shock, it usually happens very quickly, so I found myself holding my breath behind the mask.

Bill nodded at Rob. "Cut. She's ready."

Rob glanced at me. "Whisper a prayer, Carl. I have."

"So have I."

I watched intently as he deftly began the procedure, making a longitudinal incision in the lower abdomen.

Rob glanced up. "No time for a bathing-suit horizontal incision. This baby has to come out."

As he opened the abdominal wall layers, I held retractors to better expose the wound for visualization. He quickly opened the uterus and was rewarded with a large gush of blood. I grabbed the suction as he tried to gain better exposure.

Bill interjected, "You better hurry. BP 85 systolic, pulse 110 but weak and thready."

Sweat fogged Rob's glasses as he turned to the circulating nurse to remove and clean them. She wore a scrub suit, but no sterile gown or gloves were necessary for her job. She quickly had them back on his face.

The bleeding was steady now as we finally visualized the problem. "Abruptio placenta," Rob announced. "Fifty percent detached already." He cut the cord and handed me the cyanotic infant.

I immediately took her to our new fetal resuscitation table with built-in radiant warmer.

Candice assisted him as he removed the placenta that had prematurely started to separate. With the blood loss controlled, he sighed in relief as her BP slowly made its way back up to systolic pressure of 95 with a heart rate down to 100.

Turning to me, Rob asked, "How's the baby?"

I had just suctioned amniotic fluid and blood from the nose and mouth and noted a feeble respiratory effort. I turned the baby on her side and vigorously rubbed her along the spine. Most newborns don't seem to like that much. I looked up. "Baby girl. Alive."

With my initial announcement, as if on schedule, she began loudly squalling and quickly pinked up as she struggled, arching away from my hand rubbing her spine. I added, "Also loud and complaining."

The OR team shared a tension-relieving laugh.

Rob finished suturing Sue back together while I finished my initial evaluation of little Miss Harvey. Her initial examination was A-OK. It was with relief that I turned her over to the nursery staff.

Afterward, Rob and I found Loren Harvey pacing back and forth in the large waiting room just off the lobby on the main floor. He literally ran to greet us, not relaxing until he saw our broad smiles. "It's okay? Is it?"

Rob folded his arms and nodded, waiting on me to narrate.

"Everything's fine. You have a healthy new infant daughter. Do you have a name picked out?"

"Not yet. I'm superstitious. No names until I'm sure that they're alive and healthy."

He tried shaking hands with both of us at once, repeating, "Thank you. Thank you both."

I returned upstairs to find Sue groggy but just waking up in recovery. I leaned over the cart, not knowing if she would hear me or remember. "You have a healthy six-pound two-ounce baby girl. Everything's fine."

Maybe she heard me; maybe she didn't. But I said it for myself as much as for anyone else. It was a delivery I would never forget.

Chapter 13:

Gunshots and Chigger Bites

"I've killed Mom. I just know I've killed Mom."

Until interrupted by the blood-curdling shouting and moaning emanating from my office waiting room, I felt a little smug. I was running on time for a change, working with quiet efficiency, and making rapid therapeutic decisions. Together with my office staff, we were making it all happen. And then, poof! My pleasant façade of professionalism shattered as chaos and pandemonium overwhelmed my pleasant reverie.

Dropping a chart back into the rack, I raced down the hallway to the waiting room. Christine sat at her window with a silly grin on her face while Donna stood in the center of the waiting room, surrounded by would-be helpers, doing her best to quiet everyone down.

Christine clapped her hand over her mouth, shaking with poorly disguised mirth as Donna's voice rose in a reverberating crescendo, attempting to restore decorum. "Will everyone please stop shouting and be seated. I can't help anyone in this bedlam."

Christine pushed the lower panel of the French doors open, her mouth still covered with her left hand, mumbled something about getting the wheelchair from the lab, rushed past me, and slammed the door. Even with all the noise in the outer office, I distinctly heard her cackling with the door safely closed.

I made my way to the center of the melee with the thought of helping Donna sort out the tangled and confused situation. I also wanted to see if any first aid needed to be rendered, but seriously doubted it after watching Christine's antics.

Donna had most of the snickering patients back in their seats as Christine arrived with the wheelchair. Seventy-year-old Louise Tanner held the center of attention. She glanced at the wheelchair and fell backward, attempting to land in the padded seat. Serious at last, Christine thrust the chair beneath her just in time to prevent a painful landing.

Louise sat there still moaning and hyperventilating. Harold, her twenty-six-year-old son, collapsed on both knees in front of her, grasped her right hand in both of his, and said, "I'm sorry, Mama. I didn't mean to do it."

Donna had clearly had enough by this time. She grabbed the wheelchair handles from Christine and looked Harold in the eye. "Get out of the way, Harold. I'm taking your mother to the lab, and you're in my way."

Amazed, I stood aside as Donna shoved by me with Christine running ahead to open the lab door. Our calm angel of mercy had finally lost her cool.

"Harold, you sit over there by the window until I can evaluate your mother," I said.

Harold meekly complied as I turned and rushed to the lab.

Donna already had Louise breathing into a paper bag to stop the hyperventilation. And she still had a dangerous look in her eye. Seeing no obvious signs of trauma, I stood back and observed.

Within a few minutes, Louise calmed down. Donna handed her the bag with instructions to use it again if she felt short of breath, then left, returning to the outer office. Very sober now, Christine remained behind to assist me.

Louise retrieved a tissue from her purse, cleaned her glasses, sniffed a time or two, and looked up. "Doctor, why does Donna always have me breathe into this bag when I already can't breathe?"

I pulled up a chair and relaxed. "It triggers a reflex that slows your breathing as carbon dioxide builds up in the bag. But can you please tell me what happened?"

"It's Harold. He just about brought these old gray hairs down to the grave today."

"You don't appear to have any obvious injuries."

"No. Nothing you can see. But today, I was sure my time was up. My nerves are shot."

I sat in silence, anticipating the rest of the story.

"Harold loves guns and hunting. Oh, he loves them far too much. I've asked him to give them up more times than I can count. Guns are so dangerous. Don't you agree?"

"Certainly they can be when in the wrong hands and if improperly used. But please continue."

"Sometimes I think Harold loves his guns more than me."

"Yes?"

"Don't you see, Doctor?"

"I guess not. I don't have the details yet."

"Oh. That's right. Now, where was I?"

"You were going to tell me what happened."

"That's right. And I'm glad to know you're interested. Harold loves guns too much."

I must have frowned at her.

"I'm sorry. You already know about Harold's shortcomings. You want to know what happened."

"That's right."

"Harold was cleaning one of his handguns upstairs in his bedroom while I was knitting in the living room below. He thought the gun was unloaded. Did you know that the unloaded gun is always the one that kills?" Since I didn't answer, she continued, "The *kaboom* from that 'unloaded gun' tore a hole in the ceiling and in the carpet between my feet. I nearly fainted. I couldn't breathe or talk. Harold ran down the stairs and found me at death's door."

"That's what happened?"

"That's it exactly, Doctor."

"We can be thankful you weren't really injured."

A pained expression on her face, she said, "You don't really understand. My hurt is inside. You can't see it, but it's there. He nearly shot his poor old mother in the head."

I raised my eyebrows and tilted my head sideways. "I thought the bullet landed between your feet."

Louise glared at me. "Well, you don't seem too concerned. I could have been shot in the head."

"Yes. I suppose so. I am concerned. I'm just trying to sort out the facts."

"The fact is, it's my nervous condition. I need my nerve pills refilled. *Ka-boom*, Doctor. I can still hear the *ka-boom*. I'll hear it until my dying day."

I sighed in resignation. Her former physician had given her Valium 2 mg twice daily many years ago. I was never going to get her off them. "Okay, just a few."

Louise reached over and patted my hand. "Bless you. You always know how to help me."

After Louise and Harold were on their way home, I found Christine in the lab, sipping her morning coffee and taking a break.

I sat down across the table from her. "Can you tell me something? I've never seen Donna act like she did this morning. She had no patience with Harold and his mother. What's up?"

Christine grinned. "Better be careful. It's a sensitive subject. Harold has been hanging around the office a lot. He comes in to visit Donna nearly every day. He asks the dumbest questions you ever heard. He's not exactly a knight in shining armor. I'm afraid I've teased her a little too much."

"So that's it."

"That's it, but I wouldn't mention it to her if I were you."

That sounded like a good idea. "Thanks for the warning."

***

The day finally ended peacefully enough. As the ladies prepared to leave, Donna hesitated in the doorway, a serious expression on her face. "I'm sorry about losing my temper this morning. Those Tanners are a little hard to take. I promise to be more professional in the future."

"That's okay. You both put up with a lot from demanding patients. I appreciate all you do. Besides, I never would have known how good you are at crowd control without this morning's comedy act, compliments of the Tanners."

Smiling at last, Donna said, "I bet you didn't know that in my secret life I'm a police officer and riot-control expert."

With that, Christine and Donna left together. I could hear them laughing and talking in the parking lot as I finished my last charts. I was fortunate to have such good-natured and well-liked ladies working in my office. They made all the difference.

***

Two days later, with the practice once again humming along like an efficient machine, I encountered Christine in the hallway by my office. She placed a chart in the rack outside the door of the exam room across the hall, turned, and said, "He's ready when you are."

"Did you and Donna exchange jobs today?"

"Just for this one. You'll soon know why." She hurried back down the hall, turned, and mouthed, "Have fun."

Wondering about the prank, I reached for the chart and noted the name, Harold Tanner. I had to chuckle. So that was it. I opened the door and greeted him, trying not to smile too much. "What's the trouble, Harold? What can I do for you?"

"Doc, I went fishing with some of the boys yesterday. I was eaten alive by chiggers. I need some medicine for all the bites."

"Let's have a look."

"Do you have to?"

"If I'm going to treat you, I need to know the extent of the damage."

"It's embarrassing."

"I'm a doctor. There isn't much that I haven't seen. Where are your bites?"

"On my legs."

"That should be easy. Just roll up your pant legs."

"Can't."

"Why not?"

"These jeans are too tight a fit. You wouldn't be able to see much but my ankles."

"Then drop your pants so I can see what's going on. I need to know if the bites are infected."

"Do I have to?"

"Only if you want me to treat you."

"Before I do, there's something you should know. I itch a lot when I'm wearing blue jeans. So I've got some of Mom's pantyhose on to protect my legs."

I guess I hadn't seen everything. "Okay. Take your jeans and pantyhose off."

Muttering to himself, he finally got down to his boxer shorts. He looked at me and said, "Now are you satisfied?"

I bent over to evaluate the small red and swollen lesions, quite typical chigger bites. "Is this all?"

"It's enough, Doc."

"I only see about a dozen bites total on both legs. There's no sign of infection. They really don't look that bad."

"It's obvious that you aren't the one suffering."

"Look, I'll give you some cream to apply a couple of times daily. That will help until these go away. Okay?"

"It'll have to be. You're the doctor, not me."

I got up to leave the room. "You can put your, uh, things back on."

"Wait a minute. Aren't you going to give me an excuse for a couple of days off work? I can't concentrate on my job and scratch at the same time."

Dumbfounded, I stopped with my hand still on the doorknob. "You have to be kidding me, Harold. Nobody gets off work for a dozen chigger bites. What do you take me for?"

"Aw, Doc. You can see I've got problems with itching." He nodded at his wadded-up panty hose and jeans. "Otherwise, I'd never wear these things."

"Sorry, I've done all I can for you today."

As I entered the lab, I was greeted by two very mirthful young ladies. Christine acted as spokesman. "How did it go today?"

"You know how it went."

"Did you get to see his pantyhose? He told me he couldn't get undressed because of them."

"Yes, unfortunately I saw them." Then with mock ferocity, I said, "You two had better get back to work, or I may have to send one of you to help him get dressed."

Barely able to suppress their noisy laughter, they turned and fled to the front reception area and waiting room.

I sat at the table to make a note, but hardly knew where to start. What to say about a man with a dozen chigger bites, pantyhose, and a need for time off work?

Chapter 14:

Recurrent Gall Stones

As I drove to the hospital for early rounds that bright, sunny morning, I promised myself that whatever happened, I would not miss attending church with my family that day. My patients were well acquainted with my habits and would expect me to be at the hospital. I planned to slip in, see my patients quickly, and slip back out. I relished the thought of finally getting to sit with my family during the Sunday worship service.

Eighty-nine-year old Grandma Donovan lay quietly on the cart in the ER. Brought in by her daughter and son-in-law, Lori and Jason Carpenter, she had complained of abdominal pain for seventy-two hours and had stopped eating two days ago. Although it was early Sunday morning, Lori had asked that I be paged. She had spotted my car in the doctors' parking lot when they pulled up to the ER entrance.

I glanced at my watch. Only 7:00 a.m., so I still had time to get to church with my family. I hoped.

Ann Kilgore had the chart ready for me. "Good morning. She's in room 2."

"Thanks, Ann. Do you work all the time?"

She laughed. "No more than you do."

"Okay. You've got me there."

Before stepping into the room, I looked over the chart,

noticing the temperature recorded at 103, along with Ann's note that the patient's eyes appeared jaundiced. "Good morning, Grandma. Not feeling so well, I see."

Grandma Donovan attempted a brief smile. "No, Doctor. I'm under the weather today."

Lori and Jason sat in chairs pulled up on the other side of the cart. I nodded at them and sat down on a metal stool directly across from them. I looked down at Mrs. Donovan. "Tell me about your symptoms."

Grandma sighed. "Can't they tell you? I'm feeling so bad."

"Well, they can help, but only you know how you feel. Are you able to answer a few simple questions?"

"I'll try."

"Are you having pain?"

"Yes. Right up here." She pointed to her epigastric area.

"Constant pain?"

"Never goes away. Feels like a knife plunged into me there."

"Have you been vomiting?"

"Early this morning, two times after getting up."

"Any diarrhea?"

"None. My bowels haven't moved for two days."

"You have a fever. Any idea when that started?"

Grandma shook her head, and I looked across to Lori.

"Mom's actually been ill for three days. She hasn't eaten anything for two days, other than a little soup that she immediately threw up. She's complained of constant pain the entire time but refused our attempts to get her to the hospital until this morning. The fever started out low grade last night. I also noticed that her last BM three days ago was very light colored, almost chalky."

"Lori, as I recall, your mother had her gall bladder out a few years ago. Correct?"

"That's right. She had gall stones with an infection in the gall bladder. She was super sick and had to undergo emergency surgery and was hospitalized for three weeks. Since then, she's been fine—until now, that is."

"From what you've both told me, it sounds like this started out gradually and slowly built up in intensity over the last three days."

Lori and Grandma both nodded.

"I'll try to be very gentle, but I need to listen to your heart and check your abdomen. Okay?"

Grandma again nodded.

I pulled a pen light from my shirt pocket. "First, a look with this." Shining the light in her eyes, I began enumerating my findings. "Eyes jaundiced. Throat dry but normal otherwise." Taking my stethoscope from around my neck, I listened to her. "Lungs clear in front. Heart sounds normal." I glanced at the vital signs recorded on admission. "BP 165/60. Pulse 110. Temperature 103." Very gently, I placed the diaphragm of the stethoscope over the upper abdomen, listening for several seconds. "Bowel sounds diminished." I pushed in on the abdominal wall and she flinched and pushed my hand away. "Tender in the epigastrium and right upper quadrant, but no rigidity present."

Placing my stethoscope back around my neck, I looked at the Carpenters, then at Grandma Donovan. "You definitely have an acute abdomen with jaundice and fever. This could be hepatitis, but more likely you have another gall stone in the common bile duct with fever and infection."

"But how can that be since she no longer has a gall bladder?" Lori asked.

"It's true that once the gall bladder is removed, most patients have no further problems. Unfortunately, stones can still form in the bile duct. The common bile duct drains the pancreas and liver. It's not removed during a cholecystectomy. If the biliary flow is slow, kind of like a stagnant stream of water, more stones have time to form, much like debris piling up in a stream. That's especially so if bacteria or some other process causes a low-grade inflammatory process favoring the build-up of stones."

Grandma shook her head. "I didn't know that was possible, but leave it to me ..."

I stood, pushed my stool against the wall, and pulled out my pen to write on the chart. "I'm going to order some stat blood work, a UA, and abdominal X-rays. While they're being done, I'll finish rounds, then meet you back here. While Grandma is having tests done, you two can get some free coffee in the cafeteria if you like.

The tests will take at least an hour, possibly longer. But then we should have some answers." I stopped in the doorway. "One more thing. She apparently has some type of gastrointestinal infection. I'll be starting her on broad spectrum antibiotics intravenously as soon as the blood cultures are drawn."

***

While I made rounds, I heard that a critical patient in ICU was having stat labs, EKG, and X-rays done. Only two lab techs worked the weekends, and I knew my hopes of Sunday morning church with the family no longer existed. It was already 9:02 a.m.

I took a deep breath, sat down in the ER doctors' dictation room, and dialed the phone. "Hello, honey."

Before I could say another word, Janet's pleasant voice came over the phone. "Hello. Let me guess. You're tied up with an emergency as usual."

"Unfortunately, yes. I'm really sorry."

"It's okay, dear. Is anyone I know seriously ill or injured?"

"It's Grandma Donovan. I think she has a biliary infection and we're waiting on tests. A sick ICU patient came first, so you know what happens next."

"I know. I'll say a prayer for Grandma Donovan at church. She's such a dear lady."

"Thanks for understanding. I hope to be home in time for lunch."

Hanging up the phone, I sat drumming my fingers on the dictation desktop. There would still be a wait.

***

At 10:15 a.m. Sally Walker, the weekend X-ray tech, brought the films over for me to review. "Sorry to be so long. We had an emergency in ICU this morning."

"It's okay, Sally. At least you have them here now."

She hung them in a row on the view boxes in the dictation room. "Are these okay for you? She couldn't hold a deep breath for me. Said it hurt too much."

"They're fine. Her chest X-ray looks normal. No sign of free air, but you really couldn't sit her up to be sure, could you?"

Sally shook her head. "Sorry."

"The abdominal films show an ileus, not much moving in there, but no real obstructive pattern." I continued to study the films carefully. "Wait. What's this?" I pointed at a rounded lucent object, about 2 cm size, with a partially calcified rim in upper abdomen.

Sally nodded. "I know. I saw that earlier, but I'm not sure what it is."

"From the location, I'd say she has a calcified gall stone in the common bile duct obstructing most, if not all, of the bile flow to the intestine. That would explain her illness. I'll see if the blood work corresponds with a diagnosis of biliary obstruction with ascending cholangitis and sepsis. Thanks for your help, Sally."

***

Later that morning, the laboratory data indeed confirmed my suspicions. A WBC of 28,000 with an acute left shift, meaning increased polymorphonucleocytes, indeed pointing to an acute inflammatory process, one consistent with ascending cholangitis, infection of the common bile duct. The liver functions were consistent with an obstructive process with no signs of acute hepatitis. Hence, the back-up of bile in her system with early jaundice manifested first in the whites of her eyes was likely due to blockage in the common bile duct. Although septic, she showed no signs of acute delirium, which many elderly and acutely ill patients experience. I returned to the ER to consult with Grandma and her family.

I found the Carpenters in the hallway and spoke with them first. "The good news is that we have a working diagnosis of biliary duct obstruction and infection. She is septic and will have to be admitted. Hopefully the pain medication I ordered earlier this morning will keep her comfortable. The stone I see in the X-ray of the abdomen is fairly large. If it's lodged in the common bile duct as I suspect, I doubt that it'll pass spontaneously. She'll probably require surgical intervention."

After answering their questions, I motioned them to follow me. "Let's go give her the news and check with her about a surgical consultant."

***

Following extended explanations and discussion, I obtained permission to call Rob Hendrick in for surgical consultation. If the stone didn't pass soon, she would likely require early surgical intervention. (In those days, ERCP to extract biliary stones was in its infancy. It wasn't an option at that time.)

Grandma was taken to surgery where the stone was extracted during an open procedure. I assisted Dr. Hendrick and watched as he retrieved a large stone with a lot of sludge from the common bile duct.

Fortunately, she made an uneventful recovery and returned to her own home.

***

Two years later, Grandma Donovan developed another common duct stone with obstruction and ascending cholangitis infection. She required open surgery by Dr. Hendrick to remove the stone and relieve the newly developed obstruction. Grandma faced that challenge like she did everything else in life: it was just another obstacle to be overcome. Ultimately, she did very well and soon returned to her usual state of good health. She was one tough, resilient lady, and one of my favorite patients.

Chapter 15:

House Call

As the last patient checked out of the office and scheduled a follow-up visit with Christine, I glanced at my watch. Another long day, 7:30 p.m. already. Donna scurried in and out of exam rooms, straightening furniture, wiping off exam tables, and emptying trash in preparation for the next day.

"Sorry for the long day," I said. "Do you know how many we saw?"

Donna stopped momentarily to do a quick mental calculation. "I checked with Christine just a little while ago, and these last four patients make fifty-five for the day. We thought you were trying for a record. By the way, how many did you see in the hospital this morning?"

It was my turn to do some figuring. "Counting Mrs. Smith and her new baby who were dismissed this morning, I saw fifteen. I guess that brings us up to seventy for the day. It may be a record."

Donna shook her head. "I don't know how you do it."

"I do it with the help of you ladies and the understanding of my wife. I'm also learning to eat lunch on the fly while I study the chart of the next patient to be seen. I'm truly sorry that you both had to work so late tonight. We started seeing patients right after 9:00 a.m. this morning. I practically inhaled my lunch and worked on through the rest of the day without a break. I hope no one felt short-changed or rushed. I always feel in a hurry, but I try not to let it show."

Donna laughed. "No one complained about not getting enough time. The sick add-ons to the schedule don't expect a lot of your time, at least most of them don't. You don't rush them as much as Christine and I would. And we don't have families waiting on us at home."

"I'll try to do better tomorrow. When this current flu season is over, it will surely slow back down to thirty-five or forty a day. We did see a lot of work-ins the last two hours. I believe every one of them had either a viral URI or influenza."

"I know. I hope the flu vaccines we took in September are effective. From the looks of these people with the flu and their constant hacking coughs, I sure don't want what they have."

Christine approached from the far end of the hallway. "Doc, did you remember that Bonnie Newton is here to talk with you about her mother, Sandra Jackson?"

I took a deep breath. "No. I'm sorry, but I forgot all about it."

"Well, you better get prepared because she just got here. I promised to call her when we were down to the last patients."

"Okay. Tell her I'll be right there."

Donna returned to her last-minute office cleaning as I followed Christine down the hall, feeling a little like a condemned man going to his fate. Would I never get home at a decent hour?

I felt a little guilty for wishing I could avoid the whole thing by a quick escape via the back door, especially when I saw her seated alone in the waiting room, staring out the front window at the swirling snow illuminated by the streetlight. She was bundled up against the cold winds of January, still wearing her scarf and gloves. Bonnie was a gracious and caring sixty-four-year-old with an invalid mother to care for in her own home.

I took a seat near her and collected my thoughts. "Hello, Bonnie. How's your mother doing?"

She managed a half-smile. "Not good, Doctor. Not good at all." She hesitated. "I'm sure you know that's why I'm here. I hate to trouble you this late in the day, but is there any way you could come by the house and see her now?"

I hoped she didn't notice my reluctance. "Sure, I'll come by shortly. We're just finishing up here for the day. I'll only be a few minutes."

"That's fine. Very good of you. If you'll excuse me, I need to get right back. Roger is watching her by himself, and you know how nervous and squeamish my husband can get when anyone is sick."

Bonnie let herself out the front door. Her car lights lit up the now otherwise darkened waiting room as she backed her car up and turned into the street. Christine had just flipped the wall switch, and I continued to sit in the darkened room.

The ladies started out the front door and noticed me still sitting there. "Are you all right?" Christine asked.

I sighed. "I'll be okay. Just resting a minute. It's been a long day."

"I just turned off the coffee pot in the lab," Donna chimed in. "There's still about three cups of hot coffee left in it from when you brewed it a couple of hours ago. You look like you might need it."

"Thanks, ladies. You go ahead. I'll lock the front door after you get out. I think I'll take your advice and have one more cup before I leave."

They waved and Christine said, "Everything else is locked up, and the lights are all off in the exam rooms. I just checked. And you take care of yourself. We don't want you to get down. We really do like working here, late hours and all."

I waved, got up and stretched, locked the front door, checked the thermostat in the hallway, and made my way to the coffee pot in the lab. I could use another cup or two before making the house call to see Sandra Jackson.

***

The Newtons lived just outside town on two acres carved out of the old family farm. Snow had piled up around the red-brick house as the winter storm intensified. Just able to see the outline of the recently shoveled walk, I made my way to the door, holding tightly to my hat as the wind tugged at it. I hesitated at the entrance, temporarily blinded by a whiteout as wind whipped the rapidly accumulating snow from the eaves all about me.

Before I could ring the doorbell, Roger swung the door open. "Come on in, Doctor."

I tried to stamp the snow from my shoes.

"Don't worry about it. I've been tracking in all afternoon. Been trying to clear the walks. Finally gave up."

The warmth in the small entryway felt good. I looked down at water puddling on the tile floor from my thoroughly soaked shoes. "Sorry."

"Never you mind. We're just glad you came."

I slipped off my shoes and left them by Roger's boots on an already soaked mat. "Is Sandra worse?"

"Sure looks like it to me. I'll let you be the judge though. Come on in."

I followed him through the living room into an adjoining family room with a view of fields of white. Rows of harvested corn stalks poked above the snow in windswept areas, just visible in the glow of security lights on the old barn.

A metal-framed rollaway bed occupied the center of the room. A couch, coffee table, television, and other furniture had all been pushed out to the walls, except for two kitchen chairs that had been brought in and placed at the bedside.

Bonnie sat in a chair at the head of the rollaway with a care-worn smile as she pointed to the chair at the foot of the bed.

"Excuse me, Doc," Roger said. "I'll go put some coffee on. It's a cold, blustery night and it'll warm you up before you have to go back out in the snow."

I turned my attention to the bedridden invalid before me as I took my seat. Sandra had once been a robust, gregarious woman—full of life, a born leader of her church ladies' group. Now she laid curled up in the fetal position, loose fragile skin draped over a frail skeletal body. With drool oozing from her sagging lips onto her neck and pillow, she seemed to be only a shadow of her formerly healthy self. Occasional gurgling sounds accompanied by feeble coughing paroxysms revealed that she still lived.

Bonnie cleared her throat, swallowed, and reached over to pat her mother's shoulder as we talked. "I need help deciding what to do."

I nodded, encouraging her to go on.

"My brother and sister mean well, I'm sure, but they aren't much help when it comes to caring for Mother in her present condition. One day they want me to put her in a nursing home for comfort care, and I think to ease their consciences for not helping more. The next day they want all the stops pulled out and everything possible done to keep her alive a little longer. They don't really know what they want, but they're good at telling me what to do."

"Are they taking turns with you at all in providing care?"

She raised her eyebrows and rolled her eyes. "I thought you were acquainted with my siblings."

"Okay, I guess you and Roger are on your own in regard to her care."

"That would be an accurate statement. I have decided as the oldest child and POA to just do what I believe is best, regardless of any protests from the rest of the family. My two daughters live about an hour away, but they are supportive. I would like for you to check Mother once more and tell me what you honestly think. Please?"

"Certainly. Haven't I always been straight forward with you?"

"Yes, you have. I'm just terribly anxious and conflicted."

"First, let me go over a few things with you. How long since she's seen the neurologist, Dr. Marshall?"

"Mother hasn't been out of my house for six months, not since the last time you were here. She still talked a little and was able to sit up by herself then. The last several weeks have all been rapidly downhill. She hasn't said a word for a week now and doesn't seem to hear when we talk to her. I gave her a little Jell-O and some puddings until twenty-four hours ago when she stopped trying to swallow."

"Did Dr. Marshall change any of her medications for Parkinson's at the last visit, or by telephone, since then?"

"No. He said there wasn't much else to do for her except keep her as comfortable as possible. Now she can't even swallow the medicine he prescribed. That's the essence of my dilemma, and she has a terrible cough. Last night she had a fever for the first time."

"Has she ever told you what she wants done regarding end-of-life issues?"

"That's part of the problem with my siblings. Mother didn't write anything down. She was superstitious and thought that would bring on ill health. She just told me what she wanted."

"And that was?"

"She doesn't want to be on a ventilator or other machines to keep her alive unless she has some quality of life left. And you know Mother turned down a feeding tube when she saw Dr. Marshall last. Personally, I believe she's near the end. She seems to have given up, but I want your opinion. If you say we've done enough, I'll say so be it, and deal with my family and any objections they may have."

I carefully examined Sandra, noting her lack of responsiveness, her hot flushed face, the sunken eyes, the mouth full of thick secretions, the rattle in her upper airway, the crackling rales of pneumonia in the base of the right lung, the irregular beating of her heart, and her thin, rigid arms and legs. She made no effort to communicate and appeared completely unaware of her surroundings. I estimated her BP to be at least 90 systolic by the strength of her pulses, but I skipped actual measurements due to her fragile skin, which bruised and tore with the minor trauma of simply turning her body in bed to complete the examination.

Roger returned to the room with a china coffee pot, cups, and saucers on a silver tray. He gave Bonnie a cup, then extended a cup to me. "Do you want cream or sugar, Doc?"

"Just black, thanks."

Roger poured his own cup and added cream, then pulled up another chair by Bonnie to hear what I had to say.

I hesitated until Bonnie said, "Well?"

"First, I want to say that you have taken very good care of your mother. Despite her fragile skin and inability to help herself, there isn't a sign of a bedsore. You've obviously changed the pads beneath her many times. The air mattress has also helped relieve pressure, but your care is what's made the difference."

"I couldn't bear to send her back to the nursing home. The last time she was there for rehab, she came home with two bedsores that took forever to heal."

"How often did you turn her? It must have been very frequently."

Roger spoke up. "Bonnie doesn't say much, but she turns her mother every two hours by the clock. I ought to know. The alarm keeps waking me up all night long."

"Wow. That's dedication. I could tell by her condition that she's had top-notch care." I looked from him to her. "But now, what's to be done? That's the real heart of the matter."

Bonnie leaned forward in her chair. "Please go on. What do you think?"

"Basically, there are two choices. I don't believe you'll want this first one done, but I have to give it to you as an option. I believe she has pneumonia, dehydration, and sepsis—a type of blood stream infection. The only way to reverse this is to hospitalize her, give IV antibiotics and fluids, and hope for recovery. In a best-case scenario, she could maybe get back to her baseline functioning, which is very precarious at best. Bedfast patients frequently die with pneumonia from lack of mobility."

Bonnie was already shaking her head. "What is the other option?"

"Keep her home, keep her as comfortable as possible, and be with her as she crosses into the next world."

"Should you give her antibiotics or any other medical treatments at home?"

"I could give her antibiotic injections here at home, but I doubt that it will make any real difference. Since she has ruled out a stomach tube for feeding and medication, antibiotics alone will not reverse dehydration and impending kidney failure."

"I have to ask a couple of questions so I can tell my siblings that we already considered everything possible. Mother refused a stomach tube, and I have no desire to force one on her. But as POA, I could ask you to put a tube in, couldn't I?"

"You could, but I wouldn't really want to do it against her known wishes. Unfortunately, she has nothing in writing. I can tell you some of the pros and cons of an NG, or nasogastric tube, so you can answer your family's objections if you decide against it."

"That would be helpful. Wait until I get a pencil and pad of paper."

When she was ready, I continued. "First, we could carefully hydrate her with an NG tube. You could also crush up medications, put them in a liquid slurry, and administer them via the tube. We could start liquid feedings from commercially prepared sources to give her calories. Improving nutrition always goes a long way in favor of survival. We could conceivably even give her antibiotics via an NG tube. Those are the main factors in favor of using a tube."

"I think I understand. What about the negatives?"

"There are a number of complications that go along with stomach tubes, even if they are put directly in the abdominal wall bypassing the nose and esophagus. In either case, stomach tubes do not prevent aspiration in bedfast patients. Reflux from the stomach can still occur with aspiration into the lungs and pneumonia. Reflux can occur with direct abdominal-wall-type tubes or NG tubes. Also, NG tubes can predispose to sinus infections. An NG tube can cause nasal and esophageal erosions and bleeding or infection from local injury. You would need a visiting nurse to help be sure it stayed in the right position. If it comes out, it requires careful replacement. If put into the trachea by accident, and believe me it can happen, it can be catastrophic if fluid is accidentally forced into the lungs."

I looked her in the eyes. "Finally, the biggest problem is that it won't do anything for her mobility with her advanced stage of Parkinson's disease. Any improvement would be very temporary. It wouldn't do anything for her quality of life and might just make her more miserable. In a worst-case scenario, with one of the complications I mentioned, an NG tube might even hasten death."

The room was silent as Bonnie and Roger sat looking at Sandra lying helplessly in bed.

Respecting their need for reflection, I turned to look out the picture window at the still-raging snowstorm. Potentially a dangerous winter storm, it remained awesome in its majestic fury. Wind whistled down the chimney as swirling snow briefly blotted out the field. When it cleared, new drifts formed as if by magic with each sweep of the wind. I was vaguely aware of the low voices in earnest conversation and turned back around when the murmuring stopped.

"Dr. Matlock, we really appreciate you coming to see Mother

at such a late hour and in a terrible storm. I've decided to keep Mother at home. I'm sure you're right that she's near the end of her life." She looked over at Roger and took his hand. "Roger's such a dear. He's in agreement with providing care for her here until she's gone. I don't know what I'd do without him."

Roger flushed with embarrassment and looked down at the floor.

"He's a good and generous man, Bonnie."

"He did have one suggestion, and I believe it will help me with my family, that is, if you agree. I know it's unlikely to help, but would you mind giving Mother antibiotic injections? It might help, and my family is more likely to accept my decision without a big fight if something is being done to counteract the infection."

I reached for my bag. "I believe I can do that for you. I just happen to have a vial of penicillin in my medical bag. I brought it from the office, just in case."

After I gave the injection, I prepared to leave. Roger accompanied me to the door and retrieved my coat and hat from the hall closet. "Make sure that you keep the penicillin in the refrigerator," I said. "I'll swing by in the morning to see how Mildred is and give her another shot. If that goes well, I'll see if Donna can give her another dose after office hours tomorrow. She's good to help me that way. We always bring along a vial of adrenaline in the unlikely event that someone has an allergic reaction."

"Doc, I can't tell you how much this means to me. I've been worried about the load Bonnie is carrying. I know that the worst is ahead for her when Sandra passes, but I also know that you gave us a lot of relief when you didn't accuse us of neglect tonight. Bonnie didn't tell you, but that's exactly what her brother and sister did recently. Sad thing is, they won't lift a hand to help."

Unbelievable. "Neglect? No way, Roger. I've seldom seen a bedfast patient get better care than Sandra has received right here. If anyone says anything different to you, send them to me. I'll set the record straight."

A short time later, the lights of my car pierced the darkness and the swirling snow as I headed home. My wife would have my food keeping warm in the oven. She well knew the kind of life I lived.

I regretted missing the time around the table with my family, but I was glad I had been able to help Bonnie and Roger.

***

I wasn't surprised when Art McKay woke me in the wee hours of the morning three days later. I quickly picked up the phone in the darkness, not wanting to awaken the family.

Art's voice came over the line. "Doc Matlock, this is Art."

"Go ahead. What's up?"

"I'm out at the Newtons. Sandra Jackson just passed. I understand you were her doctor. Do I need to call the coroner, or can you sign the death certificate for me in the morning?"

"I'll be glad to sign it for you in the morning. By the way, how are the Newtons doing?"

"They are very accepting of her passing. They're good folks and took wonderful care of her for the last several years. I don't detect any regrets, just relief that Sandra's long battle is over. Well, get back to sleep. See you in the morning."

I hung up the receiver and took Art's advice.

Chapter 16:

Seizures and a Wild Ride

"**D**r. Matlock, emergency room stat. Dr. Matlock, emergency room stat."

The blaring calls over the hospital PA system stopped me in my tracks. I had not slept well since Art McKay awakened me advising of Sandra Jackson's death, but I had somehow managed to finish morning hospital rounds. I had my finger poised to switch off the light beside my name, the one alerting the switchboard operator that I was in-house. That was when that harsh overhead page stopped me cold.

Instead, I wheeled around and double-timed back to the ER, threw my coat and hat over an empty chair by the nurses station, and ran into the large trauma and resuscitation room where Ann Kilgore motioned frantically for me.

A cyanotic, unconscious child lay supine on the cart while Dave, an EMT with the fire department rescue unit, attempted to suction bloody drool from the tightly clenched teeth as he lifted the edge of the pediatric oxygen mask. Meanwhile Ed, a second EMT, held a violently shaking left arm while Betty, the ER charge nurse, did her best to start an IV.

I instantly recognized five-year-old Debbie Charles. Her beautiful blond curls, now saturated with sweat, adhered tightly to her head and her face was in total disarray while her little body shook uncontrollably with generalized seizures.

I experienced a flashback to two weeks ago. Bernice Charles, her mother, had brought her in for a routine physical following her birthday. Her angelic face, with beautiful deep brown eyes and rosy cheeks, was wreathed by bouncing blond curls as she bobbed her head up and down telling me about her new puppy. Unlike most five-year-old children, she had no fear of the doctor. With her exam completed, she had reached to be picked up. Before I handed her to her mother, she had planted a kiss on my cheek. Now I watched as her little body continuously convulsed on the big cart that made her look so small and vulnerable.

Fearing for her life, I stood briefly paralyzed before my training thankfully came to the rescue. Lifting her left wrist, I noted that she indeed had no visible veins, even with the tourniquet around her upper arm. "As I recall, she weighs forty-four pounds, about twenty kilograms. Give phenobarbital in a starting dose of 100 mg IM while we try to get a vein. "

Ann Kilgore soon had the phenobarbital drawn up and injected into the right thigh.

While we continued to frantically search for a vein, the convulsions slowed and eventually ceased altogether. Her mouth relaxed to reveal a bleeding deep bite on the tip of her tongue. Dave applied mild pressure with a saline moistened 2x2 inch gauze pad while continuing to hold the oxygen mask over her nares.

Debbie's little body relaxed, then shuddered once as she took a deep breath and slowly resumed a normal breathing pattern. The cyanosis resolved. Betty finally got an IV placed and secured with an arm board taped in place to prevent accidental dislodgment of the small-caliber IV catheter.

A brief assessment revealed the neck to be supple, ears and throat normal following suction, chest clear, heart rate and rhythm regular, abdomen and extremities without signs of trauma. She remained unconscious in a postictal state as expected following status epilepticus seizures.

Dave and Ed were EMTs with the Glen Falls rescue unit, and they had been first on the scene. Betty took a vial of blood to the lab for analysis as they remained ready to help.

After completing my initial assessment, I asked, "What's the story, fellas? Were you able to find out much?"

Dave, the head EMT, acted as spokesman. "You know how it is, Doc. The household was in pandemonium. The Charles family lives about seven miles out in the country, and with the developing weather situation, it took us about thirty minutes to get out there. All Mrs. Charles could tell us was that she had one brief seizure, but just before we got there, this status seizure started. It's been going on for about thirty-five minutes now. Roads are icing over with the freezing rain on top of the snow. We couldn't get here any faster."

Ed nodded. "A couple of neighbor women were there with them. Everyone was talking at once, trying to help, I suppose. I think at least the neighbors will help her get here. Her husband has their truck at work and the family car is in the shop for repairs. At least, that's what they seemed to be saying."

Ann Kilgore came back into the room. "Mrs. Charles is here now. She's beside herself, crying, and collapsed in a wheelchair in the hallway outside the ER. I tried to tell her that the seizures had stopped, but I don't think she heard a thing I said. You'd better go reassure her or we'll have her as a patient next. I'll stay here with the boys while Betty sees to the other patients. If anything happens, you can be sure I'll call for help."

"Thanks, Ann. I'll be back as quickly as possible."

I hurried to the hallway and found Bernice Charles, head bowed and weeping uncontrollably, just as Ann had encountered her. I knelt by the wheelchair and placed my hand over her right hand, which gripped the arm of the chair. Her knuckles were white from the death-like grip. "Bernice."

She looked up slowly.

"Debbie is stable now. No more seizures. Her color is good. Vital signs stable."

She looked at me as if in a fog. "She's better? Alive? You won't hold anything back from me, will you?"

"Of course not, Bernice. Have I ever been untruthful with

you?"

"I'm sorry. I didn't mean anything by what I said. I can barely think. I thought she was dying." With that, a fresh deluge of tears coursed down her cheeks and her voice wavered. "Can I go see Debbie?"

"In a minute. First, I need you to tell me what happened. Has she been sick since I last saw her in the office?"

Bernice considered that. "I'm trying to think of anything that might help. And no, she hasn't been sick that I know of. I called her for breakfast and heard her making a lot of noise in her bedroom. When I went to see about her, she was still in bed, shaking all over, bumping the wall with her arm, but out like a light."

"So no fever or cough the last day or so?"

"No. Nothing unusual."

"Any injuries?"

"No." She hesitated. "Well, come to think of it, she did fall on the cement drive a couple of days ago and bumped the back of her head. She had her sled out and was pulling her doll through the snow. My husband, Larry, was home after work shoveling snow and saw it happen. He got to her right away. She wasn't knocked out but did say her head felt funny for a little while. We didn't think much about it because she seemed okay at the time and went on playing after a few minutes. Could that have anything to do with this?"

"Maybe. Minor head injuries can occasionally cause symptoms later."

"Should we have brought her to see you right after the fall?"

"You say she acted normal after a few minutes and went on playing?"

"Yes. Exactly. But now I feel like a bad mother."

"Don't blame yourself. If she acted normal, she undoubtedly would have had a normal examination. My only instructions would have been to watch her closely the next few days. Besides, that may or may not be the cause of the seizures. I think we've gone over this before, but do seizures run in your family or your husband's?"

"Not that we've ever been told, but now I'm sure we'll do more checking. Can I go see her?"

"In just a minute. I'll go check on her first. The nurses were getting her into a dry gown. Her clothing was wet with sweat from the seizures."

Within minutes, Mrs. Charles was seated beside the cart where Debbie lay, still unconscious, hair smoothed out by Ann's ministrations, but afebrile and breathing normally now. My extended examination had been unrevealing and lab studies still were pending.

Ann summoned me to her desk. "I've been monitoring the weather on NOAA radio. The ice storm is causing havoc, and county north-south roads are quickly becoming impassable. They just broadcast an alert that the sheriff is ordering all county roads off limits except for emergency vehicles. A number of traffic accidents have already been reported. Now we have ice alternating with snow creating whiteouts."

"What are you suggesting?"

"Only that if you decide to send that child to Indianapolis, there won't be a better time than now."

I pondered my options for a moment. "I agree. I'm still not sure this is a post-traumatic seizure due to a recent minor head injury. I didn't give her a full loading dose of phenobarbital, and maybe the seizure was about to stop anyway. She's still postictal, responding some now, trying to wake up but obviously confused. I'm just as concerned as you are. I'm afraid she will go back into status seizures. When I saw her two weeks ago, she was the picture of health."

I stood and pushed my chair back beside Ann's desk. "I'm going to check her once more. Would you please get Riley Hospital in Indy on the line for me? I'll need the pediatrician on call."

Ann smiled. "Consider it done."

Within minutes, she had Dr. Hann, the on-call pediatrician on the line. I quickly summarized the case and asked, "Would you be able to accept her as an emergency patient today?"

"We have a few beds open and will be happy to take her, that is, if you can get her here. This latest winter storm has really snarled traffic downtown. How are the roads in your area?"

"Not good, but the EMTs assured me they will get through."

"Do you have paramedics to come with her?"

"We don't have any qualified in our county yet, Dr. Hann. I'm planning to cancel my office. No one can get there now anyway.

I'll ride in with them. I'll be in touch by emergency radio with your ER if anything else happens on the way."

"That's great. I'll personally meet you when you arrive. Thanks for your dedication. Have them call me the labs directly when they're completed. That'll be a great help."

"Thank you, Dr. Hann. Debbie Charles is one little sweetheart. I'm glad to accompany her."

***

Minutes later, I had Christine on the phone. "Hello. You probably know why I'm calling."

Christine laughed. "I can guess. You're going to be late."

"Not quite. Have you had our NOAA radio on?"

"No. Why?"

"The weather situation is rapidly deteriorating. The sheriff is going to close the north-south roads." I then went on to explain the situation with little Debbie Charles. "So you see, we have to cancel the office today anyway."

"Right. There's no one here yet. I doubt that many would come if we stayed open. Don't you worry. Donna is standing here straining to hear every word. We'll cancel everybody and head out of here."

"Be careful. The roads are treacherous."

"We know. Donna picked me up so we could come together for safety. We've got snow shovels and emergency supplies in the backseat. We grew up in the Midwest, you know."

"If it gets too bad, just camp out in the office overnight."

"Are you kidding? We'll get home one way or another. Donna can stay with me tonight if it gets too bad. It's only five miles to my house."

"Okay. Hopefully we can get back to work tomorrow."

***

A few minutes later, the ambulance with me aboard eased away from the ER. Ed drove while Dave and I sat beside the cart

127

monitoring Debbie. Ed called over his shoulder, "I'm going to run red lights and sirens. Okay, Dave?"

"Good idea. We'll be hard to see in this storm. Maybe that'll help. I can see that not many have got off the roads yet as ordered by the sheriff's department."

"Nah. Cars are out on the roads like it's a holiday," Ed called back through the window. "Actually, I just heard from control that most of the factories are sending people home early because of the worsening weather." He had stopped at the Main Street exit from the hospital before merging into traffic. "Hang on. Here we go."

With that, the flashing red lights cast an eerie glow on the houses and businesses streaming past as we gathered speed in the somber gray of the early morning overcast skies. The noise of sleet hitting the roof and windshield joined with the wail of the siren once we were safely away from the hospital quiet zone.

Thankfully, our patient rested quietly, unaware of the dangerous trip she had embarked on. As the ambulance slid sideways around the next corner, I grabbed for a handrail in the ambulance, poised for the grinding crunch of smashing metal, only relaxing after we negotiated the corner without mishap.

Dave grinned at me. "You'll get used to it. Ed used to race stock cars before becoming a fireman and EMT."

"Really? Why did he give it up?"

"Too many crashes and broken bones. His bones no less."

"You're pulling my leg."

"Seriously, Doc. I'm not."

I grabbed for the handrail again as we careened sideways, just missing a telephone pole that whizzed past the side window. I glanced back at Dave, who was no longer grinning but also clawing for a handhold as he swayed sideways in his seat. "Now I believe you. He's a wild man behind a steering wheel, all right."

For a solid hour, we skidded, slid sideways, and lurched through ever-increasing traffic as we neared downtown Indianapolis. We experienced intermittent sleet, whiteouts of blowing snow, and occasional freezing rain. The stop lights were the most frightening, as the occasional car or truck, unable to stop, slid across the intersection in front of us as we plowed on through red lights. Ed only used two controls most of the time, the accelerator to speed around out-of-control vehicles, and the horn. The latter had the haunting quality of a ship's foghorn, lost in the fog and mist of a tossing sea, thus adding to the frightening din.

Ed seemed to be immensely enjoying the ride. I could tell by the happy smile on his face in the rearview mirror every time he glanced back our way. Thankfully, he was a very skilled driver, and we arrived a little queasy but still intact. He carefully killed the siren and jockeyed into the ER ambulance entrance at Riley Children's Hospital, red lights still flashing, reflecting off the glass of the emergency entrance.

Dave slapped me on the shoulder. "You did great. For a novice riding in your first race with Ed, you played it pretty cool. You can ride with us anytime."

"Do you drive any better than Ed?"

"I'm more careful, if that's what you mean."

"That's what I mean. Next time, you'll drive if I ride along."

***

When we had discharged Debbie Charles to the care of Dr. Hann and his staff, we prepared to depart once again for Glen Falls. Dave smiled at Ed and climbed into the driver's seat, placing him in the middle and me by the passenger door.

"What's the idea?" Ed said. "You know I like to drive best."

Dave shrugged. "Sorry, buddy. You had Doc too shook up."

Ed relaxed and nudged me in the ribs. "Is that all? You'll get used to it."

Dave cleared his throat. "That's only partly true. You had me shook up too. I'm the driver on snow and slick roads from now on."

Ed sat back and moaned. "You guys aren't any fun."

***

The ride back was uneventful until a call came over the two-way radio. "Glen Falls Control to Rescue 1. Come in, Rescue 1."

Ed picked up the microphone, pushed the button, and

positioned it near his mouth. "Rescue 1 en route back to Glen Falls. We read you loud and clear."

"Rescue 1, there's a 10-50 PI at the twenty-mile marker on the interstate. What is your present location?"

Ed hesitated only a moment. "We're about two miles west of mile marker twenty right now."

"Sorry to put you right back to work, but Rescue 2 is on the scene requesting help with a four-car MVA and multiple victims. You're needed ASAP."

Ed glanced at Dave and then me. We both nodded as he pushed the button again. "We're on our way, Control. ETA four minutes."

Control shot back, "Ten-four, Rescue 1."

"We still have the doc with us. Ten-four." Ed reached down and flipped the switch for red lights and siren. "I just love this. Step on it, Dave."

Dave glanced over at us. "I don't believe this guy, Doc. He's sick, isn't he?"

I laughed. "Could be, but I like his enthusiasm."

When we reached the scene, there were indeed four very smashed up vehicles with a total of three injured seriously enough to require transport via ambulance. Fortunately, none were in critical condition and we were able to scoop them up and head for the nearest hospital, which thankfully happened to be Glen Falls.

We even made the Glen Falls newspaper the next morning, as we retrieved injured people from multiple vehicles along with Rescue 2. An enterprising young newspaper reporter had been monitoring the emergency frequency and got to the accident in time to snap several pictures and get our names for the press.

The only downside was that Ed raced for the driver's seat, thereby forcing Dave and me to once more endure a wild ride careening over slick roads on the way to the ER. All the way there the lights were flashing and the siren wailing a warning into the darkening late-afternoon skies.

***

When life had returned to a more even keel a few weeks later, I was delighted to see Debbie and her parents in the office. Debbie's happy smile and demeanor had suffered no injury. Her prognosis was good after the freak accident that had caused a minor brain contusion resulting in delayed-onset seizures. Riley's neurology department would continue to monitor her for the next several years. It was thought that she would indeed do well.

Chapter 17:

Pregnancy and Shock

"The pain in my right lower quadrant feels like I'm being torn in two." Peggy Wilson, a twenty-seven-year-old RN at our local hospital, stood beside the examination table, bent over and holding her lower abdomen in obvious severe distress. "Dr. Matlock, what do you think it could be?"

"Are you having a menstrual period?"

"No, not really." She relaxed as the pain eased up. Able at last to take a seat on the table, she continued, "My last normal period was about eight weeks ago when I stopped taking birth control pills. My husband, Gilbert, and I want to start a family. We've been married for three years, and I've been on the pill the whole time. I had spotting that started about four weeks after stopping the pill, but it only lasted three or four days. Since then, I've had a little flow almost every week for a day or so. I didn't think much about it because I know that stopping the pill often leads to irregularity."

"Were your cycles regular before starting on birth control pills?"

"No, never. That's another reason I didn't think much about it. I hoped I would be regular, but I guess that isn't going to happen."

"Do you have any other symptoms, such as nausea or breast tenderness?"

"Goodness, no. I just had too much lunch before coming in

for my appointment."

"Has your appetite changed recently?"

"I seem to be hungry all the time. I thought maybe that was due to being nervous about wanting to have a baby so much."

"Perhaps. Has there been any urinary symptoms?"

"None that I've noticed."

"What about constipation or diarrhea?"

"That's another negative, Doc."

"No flu-like symptoms or fever?"

"Negative."

"You seem to be much better than when you first entered the exam room. Does the pain come and go like this all the time?"

She thought about that. "As a matter of fact, the pain only started yesterday. It lasted about thirty minutes, but it was severe. I never have abdominal pain. That's why I made the appointment. Maybe I'm just a nervous nurse who's seen too many cases of ruptured appendix."

"Well, you've never impressed me as the nervous type. As an ICU nurse, you always seem to have everything together. I've never seen you really excited when things fall apart in the ICU. When you're in pain, I pay attention. As a nurse, you know what comes next."

Peggy heaved a sigh and looked down at the floor. "I know the drill. A pelvic exam."

"Right. But first, open your mouth and say *ahh*." I briefly checked her ears, throat, neck, heart, and lungs. "Everything is good up to now. I'll go out while Donna gets you ready for the rest of the examination."

A few minutes later, Donna and I re-entered the room to complete the examination. Peggy lay supine on the cart, covered by a sheet pulled down to expose the abdomen. Donna stood at her head during this part of the exam.

I palpated the abdomen, carefully checking both upper quadrants first, and found no evidence of tenderness or enlargement of the liver or spleen. I carefully pressed in on the left lower quadrant next, avoiding the area of pain until last. When satisfied that there were no palpable abnormalities, I moved my hand to the right lower quadrant, pressing in carefully as I watched her expression for any indication of pain. Peggy normally assumed a stoical personality, and I didn't want to miss anything.

"Everything appears normal, Peggy. I'm going to step out while Donna gets your legs up in the stirrups for a pelvic."

"Okay. I do understand the need for the exam. And I sure don't want you to miss anything."

Minutes later, I stood at the end of the table, with the speculum inserted, to visualize the cervix while Donna assisted. "The cervix looks a little cyanotic. Could be a sign of early pregnancy, but not the most reliable sign. No sign of inflammation or discharge, and you have no history of pelvic infections."

"No, I sure don't."

After the speculum was withdrawn, I completed a bimanual exam, left hand on the abdomen while I pushed upward on the cervix and uterus, palpating the organs between both hands, checking for any swelling of the uterus, tubes, or ovaries. Peggy was physically fit with no abnormal belly fat, and I thought I detected a fullness in the right tubo-ovarian area, accompanied by mild tenderness. Finally, I completed the evaluation by doing a rectal exam to rule out any lower colonic mass or swelling on the right. An inflamed appendix can lie low in the abdomen with swelling and pain, but the exam was normal. The stool was brown and Hematest negative for blood.

"I'll step out while Donna helps you get dressed. When you're ready, she'll let me know. I'll be back to discuss the next steps."

Five minutes later, I sat across from Peggy, now seated on a chair, and cleared my throat. "I don't have a definite diagnosis yet. You could have an ovarian cyst along with irregular cycling after stopping birth control pills."

She nodded. "Yes. Go on, Dr. Matlock. I can tell you're worried about other possibilities. For that matter, so am I."

"You could have an ectopic pregnancy in the right fallopian tube."

"A tubal pregnancy didn't cross my mind at first, but I'm sure you're right. What's the next step?"

"We now have a urine pregnancy test that is fairly accurate. I want Donna to collect a urine and run the test while you wait."

Peggy smiled. "Okay. You're the doctor."

I continued to see patients while Donna took Peggy back to the lab where they could talk while awaiting the results. (While we had a relatively new urine pregnancy test at that time, a much more accurate serum pregnancy test awaited future development.)

I was about to enter another exam room off the hallway when Donna opened the lab door and beckoned me. "The test is finished, but I'm not sure about the results."

Both nurses waited expectantly as I looked at the urine result, which unfortunately was indeterminant. They sat at the break table in silence. I turned to confirm what both already knew. "That doesn't help much. Your uterus is definitely not enlarged, but I cannot rule out ectopic tubal pregnancy. In fact, the test may be difficult to interpret if an ectopic is present."

Peggy took a deep breath. "What's next?"

"As you probably know, we now have abdominal ultrasound at the hospital. I think we ought to see if it can help."

A short time later, Donna again motioned to me. "The ultrasound tech already went home. The best I could do is 7:00 a.m. tomorrow."

"It'll have to do. Have you told Peggy yet?"

Peggy stuck her head out the door. "It's okay. I have to work all night. I'll have the test first thing in the morning."

"How do you feel? Has there been any more pain?"

"Just an occasional twinge. Nothing like the one you witnessed. Anyway, I'll be at the hospital if anything happens. You know I'm always the optimist."

"I guess it's the best we can do, but call me immediately if you have any concerns before the test."

"Will do. Meanwhile, I'm due at work in a couple of hours. And before you ask, no, I don't want to be hospitalized tonight. See you later."

We finished what was an otherwise uneventful day at the office and prepared to lock up for the night. Donna stopped on the way out. "Let me know if Peggy has any trouble. She's a dear friend."

"Okay. I'll see you ladies in the morning."

***

I spent a relaxing evening at home for a change. My hospital census was as low as it ever got, only three stable patients to see the next day. I turned in early to catch up on sleep, hoping to get through the night undisturbed.

My pleasant dreams were interrupted by a persistent loud jangling sound. I reached over to shut the alarm off before realizing that the phone had awakened me, not the alarm. I glanced at the clock as I picked up the phone noticing the time, 3:30 a.m. I yawned, then managed to say, "Hello, Dr. Matlock here. Who's calling please?"

"This is Ann Kilgore, acting supervisor tonight. You need to get right in here. Peggy Wilson just collapsed in ICU while working. Her BP is 88/65 with a pulse of 124. She said she saw you before work, and you were concerned about a possible ovarian cyst or ectopic pregnancy. We got her on a cart after she fainted, but she looks bad."

I sat bolt upright in bed. "It's probably a ruptured tubal pregnancy. I'll be right there, but first start an IV with normal saline. Give 1000 ml as fast as it'll run in. Have the lab set up four units of packed red blood cells for transfusion ASAP. She has blood type AB, Rh positive. I just checked it yesterday and we should have some available."

"Do you think I should call in the surgery team now?"

"Yes, Ann. By all means, please do. I'll call Dr. Hendrick and then be right in myself. Could you get Dr. Johnson or someone for emergency anesthesia?"

"Consider it done. Just get here quick, Doc."

I slammed the receiver down, leaped out of bed, and grabbed my clothes from the closet. I hesitated only long enough to advise my wife of an emergency at the hospital. Used to my lifestyle, she nodded and turned over in bed, away from the light on the nightstand. I wondered if she would remember what I told her. In the living room, I picked up another phone and dialed Dr. Hendrick.

Fortunately, he answered promptly and promised to meet me

at the hospital. Peggy was a favorite with the entire medical staff because of her work ethic and winning personality, so he was doubly concerned.

***

After a flying trip to the hospital, I ran up the stairs two steps at a time, and raced for the OR on the third floor where Rob Hendrick had already started scrubbing in following a brief examination of Peggy in the hallway.

I opened the door of the dressing room adjacent to the surgical break area of the OR and called out, "Be right there. Is she okay?"

Rob looked back. "Just barely. BP 90/58 and pulse 115 now. Her abdomen is tense and tender. I did a quick pelvic with Ann's help at the bedside. I agree with your diagnosis. It just about has to be an ectopic. We'll soon know." Holding his hands above his waist after scrubbing, he entered the OR, pushing against the swinging door with his back. "She's conscious and asking for you. Hurry in. I'll need your help."

"Tell her I'll be right there."

***

Peggy had her abdomen prepped with Hibiclens soap and sterile drapes when I entered the surgery suite. Gown and gloves were donned over my scrubs, and I took my place opposite Rob Hendrick as he opened the abdomen with a scalpel.

We immediately encountered a gush of dark, non-clotting blood in the lower abdomen. As I applied suction to the area, Rob quickly exposed a right tubo-ovarian mass and began applying clamps to control the bleeding. Moist surgical laparotomy sponges were positioned to hold the colon and small intestines away from the surgical site while he continued to isolate the area of hemorrhage. Within a very short time, he exposed the ruptured right fallopian tube with a fetus partially protruding into the abdominal cavity and blood pouring from the lacerated wound. Rob applied more clamps and excised the right tube and ovary while I used retractors to more fully expose the surgical area. He then glanced up to peer at Dr. Johnson, seated at the head of the surgical table administering anesthesia. "How's she doing?"

"Very well considering the amount of blood loss, Rob. Lab is bringing up two units of packed RBCs right now and her BP is up to 98, pulse down to 105 with two liters of normal saline. I'm slowing the fluids and expect to start the blood momentarily."

"That's great. We're about finished here. I'm just going to look around to be sure there are no more areas of hemorrhage. Then we'll close."

With considerable relief, I relaxed following surgery, my own heartbeat slowing noticeably. While Rob Hendrick dictated a surgical note, I sat back in the break area savoring my first cup of coffee. Candice, the chief OR nurse, had just made a fresh pot for the day shift. They were scheduled to arrive any minute now.

When Rob finished his note, I joined him, then we stopped by the recovery room to check on Peggy who was just starting to respond as the anesthesia wore off. Feeling greatly relieved, we proceeded to the elevator to ride down to the main lobby where we hoped to find her husband.

Gilbert Wilson paced back and forth in the lobby until spotting me with Rob, then he rushed to greet us. "Is Peggy all right?"

I reached out to take his hand. "She had a rough time, Gilbert. But she's in recovery stabilizing and doing much better now. This is Dr. Rob Hendrick. He's the surgeon who performed the emergency operation. He saved her life."

Gilbert immediately began pumping Rob's hand up and down as he expressed his profuse thanks. When Gilbert calmed down, Rob explained the procedure in enough detail that he would understand. "I had to remove the right tube that was ruptured along with the right ovary. I didn't take time to try saving the ovary due to her low blood pressure at the time. She lost a lot of blood, and I was anxious to conclude the operation and get her to recovery. She's receiving at least two units of blood and may need more. I had an opportunity to examine the tube and ovary more fully after the surgery was over. I don't know why she developed a tubal pregnancy. There was no sign of obvious previous infection, stricture, or deformity. It's a mystery."

"I'm just glad it's over and she's okay. I had no idea that she was pregnant. We both thought the birth control pills had messed up her cycles. If she never has babies, I don't want to lose her. She means everything to me."

Rob nodded at Gilbert and smiled again. "If you'll excuse me, I have a full day of operating ahead of me. Dr. Matlock can answer your questions now."

We sat down at a small consultation table. I was beginning to feel the weariness and stress of interrupted sleep overtaking me. "Gilbert, Peggy should be able to have children. One ovary is plenty for future generations of little Wilsons. As Dr. Hendrick said, we saw no obvious reason for the ectopic pregnancy to form. It's a recognized risk, but in the absence of physical abnormalities, it's not likely to repeat in the future."

"I'm glad to hear that. Still, I love that girl whether she ever gives me a son or daughter."

Peggy indeed recovered quickly and was soon back at her job in the ICU. She had no complications from the surgery or the blood transfusions.

I'm happy to report that about eighteen months later, I delivered their first son, Gilbert Wilson Junior. He was followed a year later by little Gloria Jean Wilson.

Chapter 18:

Miracle Drug

"**D**on't you have anything to stop this pain?" Henry Seymour lay on his right side, legs drawn up in the fetal position and hands clasped with whitened knuckles over his loosened belt and slacks.

"Donna is preparing an injection of Demerol and Phenergan. It'll only be a minute."

Henry squinted up at me, groaning aloud and muttering profanity. The painful spasm eased a little. "Sorry, Doc. Excuse my French. But try to hurry it up, will you?"

The exam room door swung open as Donna entered with a syringe and sterile needle in hand. She retrieved a small pack containing a sterile alcohol pad from the pocket of her white smock, then turned to me. "I have one hundred milligrams of Demerol and twenty-five milligrams of Phenergan for the injection. Correct?"

"Right, and he's more than ready for it."

Donna moved to Henry's side. "Okay, Henry. Pants down. This has to go in your hip. It's a big dose. I'll be as quick as possible, but it'll hurt some."

Henry looked sour but managed to slide his slacks down, exposing his left hip. She swiped over the area with the alcohol pad and quickly injected the medication after aspirating to be sure she hadn't inadvertently entered a blood vessel.

Henry yelped, stifled another oath, then grunted his thanks.

Donna grinned wickedly. "I'm sure you're welcome." An inveterate complainer, Henry was not her favorite person.

Henry frowned at me. "She's not very sympathetic, is she?"

"Donna is a professional. She's just doing her job. I'm sure she doesn't enjoy seeing anyone suffer."

Henry groaned again as he pulled up his pants, then hugged his upper abdomen once again. "She could be a little kinder."

It was on the tip of my tongue to say, "Like you?" but I remained silent instead. Henry had made the unwritten office list of complainers. Still, I realized that he had suffered a lot with his peptic ulcer disease over the last several years.

He was a hard-driving, successful Farm Bureau insurance agent with a large clientele. He could be charming, except when he was ill or frustrated in attainment of a goal. Since he was the last patient on a Saturday morning, I took a seat beside him, waiting for the medication to work.

I heard the ladies cleaning the other exam rooms, and Henry seemed to be getting some relief. I wanted to examine him more thoroughly but decided to wait until he had settled down a little more. As I sat there, I studied his chart, recalling quite vividly all that he had suffered in the last five years:

1. Peptic ulcer disease diagnosed in 1973 and treated with the usual bland diet accompanied by liquid antacids in a combination of aluminum oxide with constipating side effects and magnesium oxide with diarrheal side effects. Duodenal ulcer visualized on UGI X-rays.

2. Acute GI bleed 1974 requiring transfusion of four units of packed RBCs. Bleeding ceased spontaneously.

3. Perforation of ulcer with localized peritonitis in 1976, requiring two weeks in the hospital, nasogastric suction for ten days, and intravenous antibiotics the entire stay.

4. Vagotomy and pyloroplasty in December 1976, during the holidays of course, so Henry would miss

little work. The vagotomy interrupted the vagus nerve supply to the stomach, thereby reducing or stopping most of the stomach hydrochloric acid secretion, while pyloromyotomy allowed for drainage from the denervated pyloric valve, the outlet valve of the stomach. At least, that was true in theory.

5. Small bowel obstruction in late 1977 due to post-op adhesions and requiring two more weeks in the hospital with NG suction continuously until four days prior to dismissal. He barely missed surgery for lysis or excision of adhesions when the NG suction finally helped resolve the obstructive process.

6. Nearly monthly visits for recurrent abdominal pain and nausea. He occasionally needed Tylenol #3 (acetaminophen with 30 mg of codeine) to control the pain.

In those days, we knew nothing of *H. pylori*, the bacterium thought to be responsible for many, if not most cases of peptic ulcer disease. At that time, peptic ulcers were equated with a stressful lifestyle, excessive aspirin, steroids, and non-steroidal anti-inflammatory drugs (NSAIDs). The type-A personality appeared to be a major contributing factor. Henry sure fit that pattern.

"Okay, Doc," Henry interrupted my reverie. "I think I can stand for you to push on my stomach now. The pain has let up a lot."

"You were in a lot of pain when you came in, so I want to quickly repeat my questions that you were unable to answer at first. Have you had nausea or vomiting?"

"A little nausea but no vomiting."

"Are your bowels moving normally and without signs of blood?"

"They're normal. Brown color. No bright red blood or black tarry stuff like when I had the upper GI bleed. I had a bowel movement last night before bedtime, completely normal."

"Did you have to take any Tylenol #3?"

"Not until this morning. I took a couple of pills about

four thirty. Like I told you before, I don't like to take pain medicine. It dulls my thought processes, not a good thing for an insurance salesman. I don't remember the last time I took Tylenol #3 prior to this morning."

I proceeded with the examination, which was basically normal after his pain was relieved. No abdominal tenderness and completely normal bowel sounds. Rectal exam normal and Hematest negative for blood.

When I returned to my chair, Henry sat up on the side of the exam table, fastening his trousers and belt. "Thanks for putting up with me. I know I'm difficult when I'm hurting, but pain is a killer. Sometimes I think I'd rather die than live with this the rest of my life. Should I see a different specialist? The gastroenterologist you sent me to tells me the same things that you tell me to do. But I didn't like his idea about a complete gastrectomy. I'm having enough trouble keeping my weight up now."

"That's what I was thinking about too, but there is a new and entirely different type of medication for peptic ulcers. I just read a review in the *New England Journal of Medicine* about Tagamet. It's recently been approved for use in the United States by the FDA. It actually reduces the gastric acid secretion by interfering with a type of histamine in the stomach. The generic name is cimetidine. It's an H2-blocker, a different type of antihistamine than Benadryl, an H1-blocker that has a different mechanism of action."

"I'm willing to try anything. The Maalox and Amphogel just upset my stomach and have done little to reverse my ulcer disease. Besides, it's either diarrhea or constipation with those meds. Yuck!"

"I don't have any samples, but I'll write you a prescription for thirty days. The recommended dose as of now is Tagamet 300 mg four times daily."

"Do they have it stocked at Glen Oaks pharmacy yet?"

"Give me a minute and I'll check with Barry House."

Within minutes, I was able to tell him that Barry not only had Tagamet but would have his prescription ready when he got to the store. Meanwhile, Eloise, Henry's wife, arrived to drive him to the pharmacy and then home.

We closed the office until Monday morning after making an appointment to see Henry for follow-up in two weeks.

***

Two weeks later, I was halfway through the day when Donna and Christine entered the lab/breakroom, where I sat reviewing a chart.

"Guess what?" Christine said. "Henry Seymour is here for his appointment."

"So?"

Donna hid something behind her back, but suddenly brought out a gift-wrapped package. "So he's not complaining for once. He brought a gift for all of us to share."

"Well, what is it?"

Christine took the lead. "That's what we're dying to know. So open it up already."

"Okay, ladies. Go ahead and tear into the package."

Christine had already started before I could finish my sentence. The package surrendered to her violent paper shredding to disclose a two-pound box of assorted chocolates.

"Just what we needed for our diets," Donna exclaimed.

Christine agreed.

"You thin ladies aren't on another diet, are you?"

"Yes. You caught us," Christine answered. "But the diet can wait until tomorrow." She picked out a large piece and began munching.

Donna finished chewing a chocolate-covered cherry and began searching for another. "What diet? This is delicious. I think I like Henry Seymour now."

I made my way to exam room 2, where Henry and Eloise greeted me. Both were all smiles. Eloise spoke first. "Doctor, this is the first time in months that Henry has been able to sleep all night without getting up to take antacids. We just wanted to thank you."

"I'm really glad Tagamet worked."

"That's my miracle drug," Henry said. "My only request is that you refill it for me while I'm here today. I feel great."

Eloise added, "Yes, and it's helped his mood also. I have a new husband."

After his checkup, I pronounced Henry quite fit, recommending a follow-up appointment for three months along with continued Tagamet. As he shook my hand, I said, "The ladies and I want to thank you for the wonderful candy. It wasn't expected but is greatly appreciated."

Henry smiled at Eloise, then turned to me. "I'm just glad to get off the girls' complainer list."

That startled me. "You knew about that?"

"I heard them whispering about it in the next booth at Barry's drug store café one day. I thought it was funny and wanted to live up to it. But now I'm glad to be off the list. Besides, it gives me a great way to blackmail them when I need a medical favor from your office in a hurry." Henry winked at me, then exited down the hall laughing all the way.

***

Tagamet was soon to be followed by a number of breakthrough medications for peptic ulcer disease. The *H. pylori* bacteria would be discovered later, thus adding antibiotic treatment to the armamentarium. That and even-newer proton-pump inhibitors to be released were a real game changer for the treatment of ulcers. Surgical modalities were never completely relegated to the past, but very nearly so. It would be several years before I treated another patient needing surgical intervention for peptic ulcer complications.

Chapter 19:

To Breathe Again

"I can't breathe. Please, I can't breathe. I'm dying." The young man lay on the ER cart gasping, hyperventilating, and extremely agitated. "You don't get it. I'm sick."

Moments later, Jerome Hayden's condescending voice came over the line. "Dr. Matlock, would you please come to the emergency room and see your patient? This kid is about to drive me crazy. This is his second trip to the ER in less than twenty-four hours, and I can't find anything wrong with him but hyperventilation."

I took a deep breath and exhaled slowly. "I'm just finishing rounds and was ready to leave for the office. Who did you say it is?"

"Martin Blackwell. You have to see this kid. I don't think he's all there. I thought at first that he had inhaled or injected some type of stimulant, but his tests are all negative. Except for hyperventilation, he's the picture of health."

"Marty Blackwell? You'd better be sure. He's not a complainer."

"I don't know about that, but he sure is a super-neurotic. One of my partners saw him during the night shift and thought the same thing. He was hyperventilating then, with all tests negative."

"Okay. Give me five or ten minutes and I'll be there."

Preoccupied by the call, I finished scribbling a note on the last medical chart, hoped it made sense, and handed the orders to Hannah Carter, charge nurse on 2 South medicine floor for the day. As I hurried to the emergency room, the idea that Marty had been in the emergency room twice and was being written off as a case of nerves troubled me. Perhaps? But I doubted it.

I made my way to the ground floor and the ER, reviewing what I knew of this young man. Had it only been four weeks ago that I last saw him in my office? Twenty-three years old, six feet three inches tall, 225 pounds of solid muscle with bulging biceps and a bone-crushing handshake, he worked as a part-time reserve police officer by night for Glen Oaks and full-time apprentice mechanic by day at Mike's Auto Repair. His winsome ways and movie-actor good looks won him the admiration of every eligible young woman in Glen Oaks. Sent by Mike, he smiled at me while Donna removed a tightly wound, bloody, grease-stained blue rag. Still dripping blood, he presented a badly mangled left index finger and said, "At least it's not my trigger finger. I can still do my police job tonight."

Marty never flinched while I injected 2% lidocaine as a digital block of the finger, placed ten sutures, applied a splint, and sent him for an X-ray. Although the tendons were intact on visual inspection and mechanical testing, I wanted to be sure there were no fractures predisposing to bone infection in the dirt- and grease-filled wound I had cleaned and debrided as much as possible.

After applying his bandage, Donna gave him an instruction sheet advising him to keep his hand elevated above heart level for the next twenty-four hours to prevent swelling and lessen the chances of infection. When I handed him a prescription for Tylenol with Codeine 30 mg, he grinned and asked, "What's that for?"

"It's for pain, of course. When the lidocaine wears off, it's really going to throb and hurt like fury."

"Will it be worse than it was before you put that numbing medicine in my finger?"

"Probably not much more, but it could be very painful."

"Now, Doc. You know I can't do police work and take that kind of pain medicine. Our town marshal, Tom Collins, has to be off tonight. It's my turn to spell him."

"I'll be glad to give you time off work for the next seven days to allow that to heal. I believe you'll find it difficult to work without pain medication anyway. The town council will have to come up with another option to spell Tom."

"You're a great guy. Thanks, but no thanks. I'll just take a couple of aspirin before work."

"I think you're making a mistake, but it's your hand."

"Right. If I need something, I know where to find you."

"Be sure and get your X-ray as soon as possible."

"Okay, but first I'm going back to clean up my mess at Mike's. It's the least I can do."

And that was Marty Blackwell, psychoneurotic to hear Dr. Hayden tell it.

I picked up his chart in the emergency room and glanced at the vital signs, all normal except for respiratory rate of 30. On entering the room, one glance at Marty and I knew something had been missed. In fairness to the emergency doctors, they didn't know this young man. He had on boxer shorts, socks, and a t-shirt. His forehead was mildly diaphoretic, and his eyes darted wildly about the room until he saw me approaching the side of the ER cart.

"Hi, Marty. What seems to be the trouble today? Dr. Hayden said that you've been here two times already."

"Yeah. I'm glad to see you. He thinks I'm a nutcase, but he's the nutcase. I can't get my breath."

"Do you mean that it hurts to breathe or that you're just short of breath?"

"No pain, really. Maybe a little muscle aching. Nothing else. But something's wrong with my lungs, and I'm too weak to walk now."

"What do you mean, 'too weak to walk'?"

"My legs gave out. They just aren't working right since this morning. They felt a little weak after I got off work last night. After I got home, I got so short of breath that I'm not ashamed to admit that I was scared. "

"When did the weakness start?"

"Come to think of it, probably two days ago. I'm a jogger, you know. Couldn't do it then. Just thought I was tired. That happens sometimes. Can you do something? I'm getting worse."

"Were you sick before any of this started?"

"Had mild diarrhea and nausea for a few days, maybe two or three weeks ago. Nothing else. Could I have oxygen? Please?"

"Sure, I'll get the nurse to set up some oxygen. But first I'm going to have her draw an arterial blood gas. It will hurt some, but it's necessary to help diagnose and guide your treatment." After a quick exam noting clear lung and heart sounds, I stepped into the ER hallway, motioned to Ann Kilgore, and asked her to obtain arterial blood gases before starting him on oxygen by nasal canula at 2 liters a minute.

Ann nodded and smiled. "I'm glad you're here. This isn't the strong kid I see jogging past my home most days. I tried to tell Dr. Hayden, but you know him. I'm only a lowly nurse, not supposed to have an opinion. I was just about to tell his father to take him on to an Indy hospital when Dr. Hayden decided to call you."

Within a few minutes, Ann had blood gases drawn from his right radial artery and rechecked vital signs. Upon returning to the desk where I was jotting down his history, she said, "His respiratory rate is still twenty-eight to thirty. The rest of his vitals are normal. What do you think is wrong?"

"Let's go back in to see him. I may need your help."

A quick general assessment with him supine on the cart noted the only abnormalities to be severe apprehension with mild diaphoresis and clear lungs with a very shallow inspiratory effort. There were no signs of blood clots in his legs. A chest X-ray done the last shift hung on the view box and was completely clear.

"Did anyone watch you walk, Marty?"

"No. I told him I couldn't."

"How did you get here without being able to walk?"

"Mike brought me last night. My dad took off work and helped me get here today. I barely got to the car with his help this morning, then he got a wheelchair from the emergency nurse after we got here. I was that much worse in just twenty minutes."

"Is the oxygen helping at all?"

"Yeah. I am breathing a little better now. Still can't get a deep breath though."

"First, I want you to sit up on the side of the cart. Ann and I are going to assist you if you need help."

Marty struggled for a brief time, then sank back on the cart. "You'll have to help me. I can't get a good grip on the rails with them down. Can't pull myself up. My arms are strong enough, I think, but my legs just won't cooperate. I can't swing them over the side to get up."

Working together, we got Marty seated on the side of the cart, his legs dangling over the edge.

"Let me see you raise your legs. Just try one at a time."

Marty sat awkwardly, leaning back, struggling to raise first his right leg and then his left without success.

"Ann is going to steady you while I check the reflexes in your legs."

Marty managed a wan smile while Ann placed her hands on his left shoulder.

I tapped his knees and ankles with my reflex hammer, then checked for abnormal reflexes in his feet. "Absent knee and ankle reflexes. No abnormal Babinski reflex noted in either foot." I completed the neurologic examination, noting intact sensation in the upper and lower extremities, as well as normal reflexes in the upper extremities. "Ann, let's get him back down on the cart." I swung his feet back up as she assisted, then made him comfortable with his head resting on the pillow, sheets pulled up.

I took a seat beside the cart while Ann stepped out to call Marty's father to the room.

"What's wrong with me? It's serious, isn't it?"

Ann ushered Mr. Blackwell into the room to hear the discussion.

I stood briefly and nodded at Mr. Blackwell, shaking his extended hand. "I believe I know what the problem is." I looked back at Marty. "You appear to have Guillain-Barré syndrome, a usually self-limited illness that follows a virus such as gastrointestinal 'flu.' The problem is a temporary ascending paralysis, usually starting in the legs and ascending to involve respiratory muscles. It may be accompanied by sensory changes such as numbness, tingling, or pain. Guillain-Barré syndrome may last for a few weeks or more. The paralysis is unpredictable, but it's usually totally reversible over time.

The problem right now is that it has ascended up to and is affecting your diaphragm, the large breathing muscle that helps the lungs draw air in as it moves up and down with a bellows-type action. It may even be affecting the chest or thoracic muscles, which also assist in respiration. You may require ventilator support, not just oxygen, before this is over. My recommendation is for transfer to Indiana University Hospital in Indianapolis for care until this has resolved." I paused to let the information sink in before continuing, "Questions?"

Mr. Blackwell asked, "You mean he is going to be permanently paralyzed?"

Patients and families never hear what I say the first time. "Not at all. Normally, Guillain-Barré syndrome reverses over time. We don't understand it very well, why it begins, why it ends, but the good news is that it usually just goes away. Someday we'll no doubt know a lot more."

"What do you mean by ventilator support?" Marty asked.

"It may or may not be needed. A ventilator entails respiratory care with a tube placed in your airway and attached to a machine that breathes for you. Hopefully, it won't get that bad. But I have to be truthful with you, it could."

"I'm breathing better with the oxygen, but I catch your meaning, Doc. I'm glad to at least know that I'm not losing my mind. And I should get well eventually. Right?"

"That's exactly right. Now, with your permission I'll call Indiana University Hospital and make arrangements for you to be transferred."

***

The call was made, and Martin Blackwell was accepted without any delay. He would be transferred directly to Indiana University Hospital's medical ICU, where one of the pulmonologists would care for him along with neurology consultation. The medics were loading him for transfer as I completed his paperwork.

Dr. Hayden approached the desk and shrugged his shoulders. "I guess I missed something, huh?"

"Yes, Jerry. I believe he has Guillain-Barré syndrome

151

following a recent bout of gastroenteritis."

He sat down in an empty chair by my desk. "Sorry. How was I to know? He sure looks healthy, like Superman."

"You would've got the diagnosis right away if you had asked him to stand up and take a few steps. But I did have an advantage over you. I happen to know this young man. He is most definitely not a complainer or a neurotic. In fact, he is very stoical. I have treated him for several injuries, and he has never even asked for pain medicine."

Dr. Hayden leaned forward, twiddled his thumbs, and stared at the floor.

I couldn't help but feel sorry for him. He was still quite young and often overly impressed with himself. "Jerry, don't be too hard on yourself. None of us are perfect, although the general public expects us to make zero mistakes. After all, doctors are only human. The redeeming quality is that we have the ability to learn from what we miss. Just be sure and listen to a patient talk, but also watch him walk before he leaves your department. You won't miss much that is serious if you do that."

"I guess you're right. It's easy to jump to conclusions, especially with hyperventilators."

"That's a danger that every doctor faces, every day he or she practices. I'm sure you won't miss the next one. Right?"

Dr. Hayden looked up, smiled, and reached to shake my hand. "Thanks. I'll remember what you said. Make 'em talk. Watch 'em walk."

Standing behind him, Ann Kilgore winked.

I smiled. "Something like that."

Chapter 20:

More Trouble Breathing

"**D**r. Matlock, you'll never guess who's here for an appointment."

"I give up, Donna. Who's the mystery guest?"

"Marty Blackwell is home from the hospital and here for follow-up. Isn't that wonderful?"

"It certainly is. It's only been about four weeks since he was admitted."

"Actually, only three weeks," Christine interrupted as she entered the break area, "and he looks great."

I chuckled. "Every young lady in Glen Oaks agrees with you."

Christine blushed. "Well, he does look great."

Donna handed me his chart. All normal vital signs and no complaints. "The internist at Indiana University Hospital told him to see you for follow-up this week. He's all set when you're ready to see him."

I took the chart and proceeded to exam room 1.

Marty stood up to shake hands with his usual iron grip, and I tried not to flinch. "Hello, Doc. Good to see you. Thanks for sending me to IU Hospital. They took really good care of me." He paused, blinking moisture from his eyes. "And thanks for not writing me off as some nutcase like they did in ER."

"I'd never do that. I know you too well. It's great to see you up going strong so soon. How are you doing today?"

"Fine. Just fine. I'm supposed to see you so I can go back to work. Otherwise, I'm totally back to normal. If you say it's okay, Mike says I can start back in the auto shop tomorrow morning. Then Tom says he can use me next week for a couple of nightshifts. He doesn't get much time off, and I'm glad to help out."

"First, let me just check you out. Stand up straight, feet together, arms extended in front of you, then go up on your toes without losing your balance."

He stood, followed directions without difficulty, and finished with a flourish, pirouetting in a complete circle with his arms extended as directed. "You mean like this?"

I had to duck to keep from being mowed down by his powerful arms. "That's the general idea. It looks like you have your balance and strength back."

He laughed uproariously. "I sure do. Go ahead and put me through the mill. I'm ready for anything you can throw at me."

I completed a general exam along with a neurologic assessment. His reflexes had returned to normal along with his strength. No sensory impairment or muscle weakness was noted. "One more thing. Step out in the hall with me and walk with one foot placed directly in front of the other without looking down."

Marty guffawed loud enough to be heard all over the office. "I'm not drunk. That's what I do to test the town drunks on Saturday night. You trying to take my night job?" Nevertheless, he proceeded to walk in tandem gait the entire length of the hallway and did it with his eyes closed.

"That good enough?"

"That's good enough. You may return to work at any time with my full blessing."

Donna already had his note prepared, just awaiting my signature. Permission slip for return to work in his hand, Marty grinned once more and saluted me. "See you all later. Thanks again."

I hurried into the break room to finish his chart and grab another cup of coffee. The office was very quiet after Marty made his dramatic exit. I was savoring the last of the rich dark coffee when Donna entered with a mirthful smile on her face. "What are you so happy about? Are you also smitten with Marty?"

"No, not really. He is handsome, but he's too much of a character for my taste. He's out in the parking lot, just outside the doorway, with a bunch of the young fellows around him, regaling them with his recent adventures in the hospital. And he's singing your praises. He's telling everyone that you saved his life."

"I wish he wouldn't do that. I didn't save his life, just made the correct diagnosis. People might think I put him up to telling that story."

"I wouldn't worry about it. Everyone knows Marty, and he's good advertisement for the office judging by the growing crowd around him."

"Okay. So be it. I just hope he gets tired of talking soon."

Donna raised her eyebrows. "Marty? Get tired of talking? Ha!"

We continued working our way through the rest of the office schedule until just after 6:00 p.m. Then I stood and stretched after finishing what I thought was my last chart—that is, until Donna handed me one more. "I thought we were finished."

"Not quite. This is a late work-in. You can blame me if you want, but Dennis Farley just walked in asking to see you. He says he can't get his breath, and he looks bad."

"That's okay. Dennis is not one to cry wolf. Do you have him ready to be seen?"

"He's undressing in exam 2. I just have to get his vitals as soon as he gets into a gown."

Within minutes, Donna handed me a set of vitals to be added to his chart. BP 168/60, pulse 102, temperature normal, respirations 24. Chief complaint: shortness of breath.

Donna accompanied me to assist as needed. Dennis was eighty-three years old and somewhat frail. He walked with a cane and a noticeable limp resulting from a fractured hip requiring replacement several years ago.

"Hello, Mr. Farley. What's the trouble?"

He extended a tremulous hand to shake mine. I noted his sweaty palm and weak grip as he attempted a fleeting smile. "Just Dennis, Doc. My friends call me Dennis. Have you forgotten?"

"Of course, Dennis. Sorry. I'll try to remember."

"That's okay. I know you're a busy man. I shouldn't be bothering you, but Martha insisted that I get something done. Tired of hearing me complain, I suspect. Wives are like that, you know."

"Donna said you were having trouble breathing. Can you tell me about it?"

"She did, did she?"

"Yes. What about it?"

"Well, she told you right, but I hate to complain."

It was my turn to smile. "You don't mind complaining to your missus."

"No, but she minds it a lot." He hesitated. "And I'm just wasting your time and mine being here."

"No, you're not wasting anyone's time if you help me out now. Will you please tell me the reason for this visit?"

Dennis sighed and took a deep breath. "I'm losing my breath when I do anything. I walk across our living room and have to collapse in a chair to rest before going into the bedroom or dining room. I can't seem to do anything. I guess I'm just no good anymore."

"Dennis, you are eighty-three now, but I'm guessing there's more to it than that. What else can you tell me besides your awareness of increased shortness of breath and weakness?"

He looked down at his hands for several seconds. "There's some bright blood mixed in with my bowel movement. I didn't want to say anything about it, but Martha insisted I tell you. I know she'll pump me with questions when I leave here."

"That's nothing to be ashamed of, Dennis. But it's an important fact."

He continued to study his hands, and I knew he had more to say, so I waited before finally asking, "What more can you tell me?"

"Look at my hands."

I looked down, not quite understanding what he wanted me to see at first. Then I noticed the large bruises on the backs of both hands as he pulled his sleeves up. "Did you have a fall, Dennis?"

"That's just it. I haven't even bumped them on anything."

I took his hands in mine and saw splinter hemorrhages

beneath some of the nails. I turned them palms up and saw how pale they were, lacking the normal reddish flush in the creases.

"It's something serious, isn't it?"

"I'm not sure yet, but let me have a better look at you. I'm going to pull your lower eyelid down to look at the conjunctiva."

"Okay, Doc. Whatever you say."

The conjunctiva was very pale, but even more disconcerting, there were scattered tiny pinpoint hemorrhages also. In fact, his entire complexion was pale when I shined a light over his face. "Open your mouth wide while I shine my light." I noted swollen gums with mild bruising and a few punctate hemorrhages of the soft palate. "I need to see your chest and back better, so let's just unfasten the snaps and slide the top of this gown down to your waist." After brief inspection, I continued, "Dennis, you have little punctate hemorrhages and larger areas of ecchymoses—or bruises—all over your back and chest. Please lie down on the cart. Donna will pull the extension out for your feet to rest on. I want to check your abdomen and do a rectal exam last. Okay?"

Dennis just grunted and nodded his head.

The abdominal exam was normal, and a rectal exam was completed with him lying on his side, feet and legs drawn upward. "Rectal exam normal except for a little blood noted. The exam is finished. You can get dressed again and then we'll talk about the findings."

Donna assisted him down from the cart, but he refused our help in dressing, saying, "I'll make it fine by myself. Just give me a minute."

A few minutes later, I re-entered the room to discuss the findings with Dennis, but he spoke up first. "I'm pretty sick, I think. What about it?"

"I'm going to be perfectly honest with you, Dennis. I don't have an exact diagnosis yet, but you are experiencing a coagulation problem in your blood. You appear to be fairly anemic, and you're experiencing little hemorrhages in the skin and soft tissues of your body. It may be quite serious, depending on the diagnosis. How long has this been going on? You had to notice all these hemorrhages for a while now."

"Maybe two, three months now. I'm not sure. To tell the truth, I was afraid of what you'd tell me, so I waited for a spell to come in."

"What made you change your mind now?"

"For one thing, Martha wouldn't quit hounding me. For another, it's getting more difficult to breathe and get around the house. I guess I'm at the end of my rope." He scanned my face, looking for some sign of hope, I suppose.

"Dennis, I would like for you to go to the hospital so we can get to the bottom of this quickly. Are you willing?"

He sat in silence for a long moment before answering. His voice cracked a little when he finally broke the silence. "I guess I don't have much choice, but I need one more night at home first."

"What is so important that you can't go now?"

"Martha doesn't know where I keep our important papers. Like, you know, my will."

"Dennis, I haven't said you were going to die. We don't even know what's wrong with you at this point."

"I know, but I have this feeling. You see, I've been praying, making sure I'm ready and all. You know what I mean?"

"Yes, I do. But I don't like to hear my patients giving up."

"I appreciate your concern, and maybe you can do something for me. I'll call you in the morning to make arrangements for the hospital. Okay?"

I took his hand to give a reassuring handshake. "Okay, my friend. Okay."

Chapter 21:

What Really Matters

Midmorning arrived the following day, and I still had not heard from Dennis Farley. I had difficulty concentrating on my work as I awaited his call, feeling that he indeed had a life-threatening medical condition.

"Christine, see if you can get Dennis on the phone. I need to see what's going on with him. He promised to call this morning so I could admit him to the hospital."

Within a few minutes, Donna came and knocked on exam room 3's door. I excused myself as Donna opened the door. "Sorry to interrupt, but you have a call on line 2."

"I'll take it in the break room." Knowing it had to be Dennis, I didn't want to be overheard.

A soft quivery voice came over the receiver. "Doc, it's Dennis."

"What's going on? You promised to go to the hospital this morning. I've been waiting for your call. We need to find out what's going on as soon as possible."

"Like I told you, I have some things to do first."

"You mean your will and important papers? Have you found them?"

"Oh yeah. I took care of that last night. Martha has everything in a folder."

"Then what are you waiting on? We need to get you in the hospital now. Today!"

"There's one thing I have to do first. Try to understand."

I waited silently as the voice on the receiver broke.

It sounded like a soft sobbing before Dennis could continue. Finally, he said, "I had to see my preacher first, had to do some praying."

It was my turn to struggle for control. "That's good, Dennis. What else?"

"I have a younger brother, a good man really, but when our mom died years ago, we argued over the inheritance. We haven't spoken for twenty years. I called him last night, and he's on his way to see me now. I asked forgiveness for my part in the argument, and he's on his way to take me to the hospital. We reconciled over the phone."

There was another long silence with subdued sobbing on the other end of the line. At last Dennis continued, "So you see why I can't go yet. I decided that there are things that really matter in life, a small inheritance isn't one of them. I'm just glad that Clarence didn't hang up on me before he heard me out. I guess we both shed tears."

With a lump in my throat, I said, "I understand. Tell you what, I'll go ahead and make arrangements for your admission. Just have your brother take you to the hospital as soon as you've had your visit." I hesitated. "That does mean today. Right?"

"Right. And please don't feel bad, whatever happens to me. I have a bad premonition about the outcome. I've already dreamed about my funeral."

"Now, Dennis. I don't want to hear that kind of talk."

"I know. Just don't blame yourself if things don't turn out so well with me. I've made my peace with God and man. I'm ready for life or for death."

Too moved to comment more, I simply said, "See you at the hospital later today." I sat for perhaps five minutes, staring out the window at the neighbor's horses peacefully grazing in the pasture.

Donna opened the door and quietly entered, sensing my mood. "Is anything wrong?"

"No. Not really. I'll tell you about it when we get a break. I just heard words of wisdom from an elderly man who is probably dying. The most important things in life do not consist of money or wealth, sometimes not even immediate health issues. Please go ahead and arrange his admission. Diagnosis: severe anemia and coagulation defect. I'll call orders during lunchtime."

Donna raised her eyebrows. "Whatever he said must have been profound."

I could tell she wanted to know more, but first I needed to return to seeing patients. She left to make the call.

***

Later that evening, following a hurried meal with my family, I sat in the dictation room on the 2 South medicine floor perusing Dennis Farley's chart. His laboratory findings confirmed my concern: WBC of 28,000 with a few possible blast cells noted, hemoglobin 6.5 with hematocrit of 20%, and a very low platelet count of 30,000. No wonder he was short of breath. His other chemistries revealed minor abnormalities, including an elevated blood BUN at 40 and creatine of 2.0, reflecting mild renal impairment likely consistent with his advanced age, for he showed no signs of dehydration on physical exam.

When I entered Dennis's room, Dennis introduced me to his brother, Clarence, and Clarence's wife, Jane. Martha sat anxiously by the head of the bed. Dennis had an IV of normal saline already running in the left arm in preparation for a transfusion of packed RBCs for the profound anemia.

He shook my hand and managed a smile. "Dr. Stanberry, the cancer doctor, has already been in to see me. You fellas don't waste any time, do you?"

"We try to take care of our favorite patients as soon as possible. You should know that by now."

Dennis assumed a look of mock seriousness. "Sure you do. Like when I waited for an hour to see you a couple of months ago. You were really quick."

I threw my hands up. "Okay, you got me there."

"Just kidding, Doc. I know you're busy all the time. Like now, you should be home with your family, not here seeing an old coot like me." He paused, dropping his bravado. "But I'm glad you're here. Doc Stanberry said something about leukemia. He used a lot of big words, said I would be getting blood and more tests. He mentioned a bone marrow test. What's that?"

I took a seat on his left side, across from Martha. Clarence and his wife were seated at the foot of the bed. "Do you want me to explain in privacy? Or do you want your family here?"

"I got nothing to hide from my family. Go right ahead and spill the beans. I can take it."

"Okay. Dr. Stanberry's note on the chart indicates that he suspects acute leukemia, probably myeloblastic type. He looked at the peripheral smear in the lab and wants to do a bone marrow test tomorrow for confirmation."

"That's the part I don't understand. What is a bone marrow test? Sounds painful."

"Well, it can be painful, but not always. It's done by puncturing into the bone marrow with a large bone marrow needle and aspirating to obtain cells for analysis. The sternum or breastbone or the pelvic bones are the ones used most often for the test. As an intern, I served with Dr. Stanberry and performed some of the bone marrow tests myself as he stood by. I can tell you that most patients had little trouble with it. Some reported moderate brief pain, others reported little to no pain. It's unpredictable. We're all different, as you're well aware."

Dennis sighed. "I can take it. I'm a tough old man. Maybe not good for much anymore, but still tough."

I patted his hand. "You'll do fine with the test. I have no doubt. Dr. Stanberry is very good at the procedure. He'll use some local anesthesia to help you with the pain."

Dennis nodded his understanding.

"Any further questions?"

Martha shrugged and no one said anything else.

"If not, I'll see you early in the morning. Try to get some rest. I've left an order for a sleeping medication if you need it."

"Okay. I'll probably take it after my family leaves."

Martha followed me into the hall. "Dr. Matlock, can I ask you another question please?"

"Sure. Go right ahead." I thought she had been a little too

quiet during the brief visit.

"This myeloblastic leukemia, are those the right words?"

I nodded. "Yes, go on."

"Is that bad at his age?"

I never tried to mislead patients or families, but I never wanted them to lose hope. "Acute myeloblastic leukemia, or just about any of the acute leukemias, are serious at any age. However, the oncologists, the cancer doctors, are continually making new discoveries in treatment regimens. Some are more treatable or curable than others. Let's wait and see what the actual diagnosis is before thinking about prognosis or outcome."

"And the bone marrow test will give that answer?"

"Yes, it should. Then we'll have more answers."

***

The next morning, Dr. Stanberry approached me in the hallway of the hospital as I began rounds. "I have bad news about your patient, Mr. Farley. I just looked at the bone marrow prep in the lab with the pathologist, Dr. Howard. It's acute myeloblastic leukemia with resultant anemia and thrombocytopenia. Very few platelets in the bone marrow. No wonder he's bleeding into his soft tissues. He has a low-grade fever this morning also, but it's probably just the leukemia. I took the liberty of getting blood and urine cultures started, but fever is a common finding with this, even in the absence of infection."

"What do you recommend?"

"I would like to have him in Indianapolis at Indiana University Hospital where I can see him every day. I'm not due to be here again for a couple of weeks. I talked to him about chemotherapy, and he seemed willing, but only if you okay it." He grinned at me. "I don't know what it is about you family doctors, but a lot of your patients don't trust me until you give the final word of approval."

I rolled my eyes. "I don't understand it either. I think he just wants reassurance that he's doing the right thing. I'll go see him right now. You go ahead and arrange the transfer. I'll be my most convincing."

***

Dennis had no visitors yet, and I sat beside the bed after examining him again. "Your color is a lot better after the transfusion of blood. Are you breathing any better?"

"A lot better, Doc." He looked steadily at me. "Tell me the truth. It's not good, is it? Doc Stanberry wants me to go to University Hospital."

I sighed. "No, Dennis. It's not. The leukemia you have can be very aggressive. But it is treatable. I believe in Dr. Stanberry. I did part of my training with him. I mentioned that last evening. He's very good. He's also a compassionate man with a high regard for his patients. He'll always consult with you before any treatment or change of plans. I believe you should do as he says."

"In other words, go to Indianapolis?"

"Exactly. Will you give consent?"

"If you think it's what I should do."

"It's what I know you should do, Dennis."

He nodded and shook my hand once more. "Thanks for caring for me. I know I'm just a stubborn old man, but I appreciate your patience with me. I'll do what you say."

***

Dennis Farley went to University Hospital but did not do well with the cancer treatment regimens. After his last treatment, he developed a bout of acute renal failure that resolved in about three weeks. Dr. Stanberry had a long consultation with Dennis, Martha, and Clarence about the pros and cons of continued treatment. In the end, Dennis decided to stop therapy and return home for his last days.

Dennis was experiencing bone pain by then, and I made several house calls to check on him during that time. He required narcotics by mouth and occasionally by injection. He appeared at peace, surrounded by family including Clarence, who assumed much of the daily care.

Four weeks after Dennis returned home, I stood in line at Art McKay's funeral parlor, waiting with my family to view Dennis. When we reached the head of the line, Martha hugged my wife while Clarence embraced me.

"Thanks for all you did for Dennis," he said. "We really appreciate it. I don't know if you're aware of it or not, but Dennis thought a lot of you. We had family devotions with him every day after he came home from the hospital, and he always included you in his prayers."

I blinked tears from my eyes. "Thanks, Clarence. I could be paid no higher compliment."

Chapter 22:

Enjoying Ill Health

Donna handed me the next chart with an evil grin. "Connie's ready to see you. She's in exam room 1." Instantly exasperated, I said, "Really? You're not joking?"

"Really. I wouldn't joke about Connie."

I sat down hard in the break room, groaned softly, and began thumbing through the chart. "What's her complaint now?"

"Her leg is jumping."

I looked up. "What in the world does that mean?"

Donna laughed. "It means that you have to figure it out. She proudly told me that we have misdiagnosed her once again."

"Please don't tell me that she has been reading her fifteen-year-old edition of *Harrison's Internal Medicine*."

"My goodness, how did you ever guess?"

"Just a lucky stab in the dark, I'm sure."

As Donna wheeled about to retrieve the next patient from the waiting room, I asked, "Do we have a full schedule this morning?"

In the doorway she looked back over her shoulder. "It's full. And I should warn you that she has her writing pad with a long list of ammunition, I mean questions. Good luck."

Another cup of coffee was poured to steady my nerves before I embarked on the trial by fire awaiting me in exam room 1. I opened her chart again, and my eyes wandered aimlessly over information I knew all too well: Constance Thorndike, age fifty-five, moderately obese, housewife with anxiety and multiple complaints. Husband Ollie Thorndike. I reread my note in the margin that he spends most of his day in the fields and in the old ramshackle barn. I admit to an unworthy thought: *I wonder why he does that?*

Five minutes passed before I saw the bottom of my cup and knew I could delay no longer. I reluctantly heaved myself out of the chair and walked like a condemned victim to his doom. "Good morning, Connie. How are you today?"

"Dr. Matlock, as anyone can plainly see, I'm not a well woman. I wish someone could diagnose my case before it's too late. I don't expect to ever see age sixty, not in my condition."

"What seems to be the trouble today?"

"This insufferable itching. It never stops." She rolled her left sleeve up to her elbow, and before I knew what she was doing, she shot her left forearm under my nose. She seemed not to notice me jerking away from what looked like a thrown punch. "Now tell me that you don't see them."

After regaining my composure, I cradled her left forearm in my right hand, minutely inspecting the forearm as I turned it back and forth. How many times had I done this at her request? "I'm sorry. I still don't see anything except excoriations where you've been scratching your skin."

She glared at me, then grabbed an object from her lap and thrust it in my face. "Then try this."

Shivering inwardly, I pulled my head back to focus on the object in her hand, then meekly nodded. "That's a nice magnifying glass." She stared at me over the rims of her glasses, and I hastened to add, "I'll give it a try."

Connie sat back and relaxed after surrendering the magnifying glass into my reluctant hands. As usual, she was winning this tug of war between us as I complied with her demands. I spent a minute or two staring through the glass at the scratched but otherwise normal skin of her forearm, hoping it would satisfy her enough to proceed to the next topic.

Finally, I pronounced my verdict. "I just don't see any parasites or anything other than all these excoriations where you've been digging at your skin."

"Humph! I expected no better from you. You're as bad as my husband. His eyes must be weak because he tells me the same thing."

"I'll be glad to send you to see a dermatologist for another opinion."

"Already saw one. Remember?"

"Oh yes. Well, how about a different dermatologist?"

"I'll have to think about it. All doctors do is take more of Ollie's hard-earned money. I never get any better."

I was anxious to change the subject. "Donna said you had a problem with your leg. Can you tell me about it?"

She pondered that for a moment. "I've told you about this before. The nerve pills you gave me didn't do a bit of good. But maybe you can tell me what kind of specialist to see next. I never get much more from you than referral to this specialist or that specialist. You'll have to get the right one sometime if we keep trying."

I dearly wanted to refer her to psychiatry, but I knew from past experience that she would blow up if I even suggested one. But wait, maybe I was the one needing a psychiatrist? I was becoming paranoid, thinking she could read my mind. Did I look guilty?

She cocked her head sideways, the way she always did before rebutting my arguments. "Now don't look at me that way, Doctor. I know what you're thinking."

Startled, I said, "You do?"

"Yes, I do. And I'm not crazy. You'll improve as you get more experience in diagnosing patients."

Speechless, I could only nod.

"Now here's what I think. I've been checking in my *Harrison's Internal Medicine*, and I believe there is a problem in my nervous system causing this leg to jerk."

I started to respond, but she simply shook her index finger in my face. "Don't tell me that book is out of date again. I bought that at a legitimate yard sale and have great faith in the contents of that old book. After all, it was written by professors of medicine, famous for their work and experience. Those old doctors knew more than you young doctors today will ever know."

I was becoming irritated and strained to keep my tone of

voice at an even keel. "*Harrison's Internal Medicine* is a highly respected textbook. I have the latest edition in my library and use it extensively. But you have to realize that treatments and diagnostic modalities change all the time. A fifteen-year-old textbook is hopelessly out of date."

"I won't argue with you. Just send me to a neurosurgeon. My reading in the book you so despise has led me to the conclusion that I need a good neurosurgeon."

I started to tell her that I didn't despise Harrison's textbook, but the dangerous look in her eye gave me pause. She had been slightly bouncing her left leg up and down during the visit, but with increasing oscillations, she now banged her foot up and down on the floor, warning me as reliably as any barometer of the approaching storm. I sensibly said, "I suggest Dr. James Lofton, renowned neurosurgeon."

"Okay. I'll give him a try."

She looked down at her list to continue, but I jumped up before she could say anything. "Excuse me while I go set up your appointment with Dr. Lofton." And I was out the door before she could answer.

I grabbed the next chart and motioned for Donna. "Have Christine set her up to see Dr. Lofton in Indianapolis. Then please get her out of here."

Donna suppressed a laugh and whispered, "I could tell she was in rare form today."

Fifteen minutes passed as I saw the next patient. When I finished and opened the door, Donna stood nearby, waiting in the hallway. "Connie says to tell you that she wasn't finished."

"What? She already killed a lot of time over nothing. What does she want to talk about now?"

"She wants to have her urine checked. She's decided a kidney infection needs to be ruled out as the source of her leg jerking. And, Dr. Matlock, you should see it jerk now. It looks like she is keeping time to bluegrass music. Listen."

A rhythmic *thump-thump-thump* came from the front of the hall, easily heard from where I stood thirty feet away. It sounded for all the world like foot stomping at a barn dance.

"By all means, check her urine and tell her to stop making that noise."

Donna shook with mirth. "You'd better tell her. I can't do it with a straight face."

The absurdity of the situation dawned on me, and I gave way to soft laughter. When I finally regained control of my emotions, I saw the door to exam 1 cracked open, an eye staring down the hallway. The stomping had stopped.

The smile on my face disappeared, and I jerked open the door to exam room 2 to avoid further confrontation with Connie. Ten minutes later, I finished treating a child with strep throat and re-entered the hallway, only to discover Donna, once more patiently waiting.

"The urine dipstick is all negative, and she still wants to see you."

I shrugged my shoulders, then resigned to my fate, opened the door to exam room 1. "What can I do for you now, Connie?"

"I want to know about my back X-ray. What did it show?"

"I went over that with you two weeks ago. Do you still have questions about the same test?"

Her foot was thumping the floor once again. "Did they X-ray all of my vertebrae or just some of them?"

Out of patience now, I simply said, "The X-ray of the lumbosacral spine with five views was totally complete and normal except for mild age-related arthritis. There's nothing else to review. I'll see you at your next appointment."

I shut the door before she could respond and double-timed to the break room.

***

Two weeks later, as I neared the end of office hours, Christine met me in the hallway. "I have bad news for you."

I lifted my eyebrows. "Bad news? We're about forty-five minutes past closing time already. What more could be wrong?"

She smiled ingratiatingly. "Actually, two things. First, remember Donna telling you she had a dental appointment at 5:30

p.m.?"

"Yes. I remember."

"Well, she already left to keep from being late. So you're stuck with me as helper."

"I'm not worried. I'm sure you can help me finish up. But what's the second piece of news you mentioned?"

"Connie Thorndike walked in before I got the door locked."

I had that old familiar sinking feeling again. "What does she want now?"

"She saw Dr. Lofton this morning and wants to tell you about the visit."

I must have looked astonished, because Christine said, "I'm not kidding you. She insists that she see you now."

I threw my hands up. "Okay. Tell her to have a seat until I finish with the last two already in rooms. I'll see her last."

Those patients were relatively quick work-ins with viral symptoms and took little time to diagnose and treat. Within a matter of fifteen minutes, I was ready for Christine to put Connie in a room. "Put her in my office where I usually do consultations."

While waiting for Christine to return with vital signs and Connie's chart, I finished my patient charts in the break room. Fifteen minutes passed, and I got up to check on Christine's progress.

Christine opened the door and entered the break room. With her left hand on her head, she extended the chart to me with her right. "Whew. I'm sorry it took so long, but I was trapped in there. She wouldn't stop talking long enough to take her temperature. But her BP is 140/88. Pulse 89. I bet mine is higher than that after listening to her complaints."

"That bad, huh?"

"Doc, you have no idea."

"Is she angry with me about something?"

"I don't know, but I don't think so. She talked in circles. I'm not sure what she wants, but she wants to tell you about her visit, I think."

Shaking my head, I muttered to myself as I proceeded to my office. *Keep calm. Don't say anything without thinking it through first. This will soon be over. It'll be time to go home and see the family.* I paused at the closed doorway, then reached for the knob, hoping that my self-talk would steel me for whatever was to come. "Hello, Connie."

She jumped up from her chair to shake my hand. "I just had to thank you for sending me to that wonderful neurosurgeon. He's a marvel if I ever met one. In less than five minutes, he diagnosed my case with authority."

Nonplussed, I could only stand there as she pumped my hand up and down.

"Isn't it just grand, Doctor?"

"Uh, sure. It's grand." Had I missed something in regard to her symptoms? Hesitating as doubts filled my mind, I finally asked, "What did he say was wrong?"

"Dr. Lofton said, and I quote, 'You have a dead brain cell.'"

"That's what he said?"

She finally stopped pumping my hand. "Yes. Now I'll be able to tell my friends what's wrong with me."

Containing the urge to laugh, I found my tongue again. "What did he say would be the treatment?"

"That's the best part of all. He said there is not a thing he, you, or anyone else can do about it. I'll just have to live with it, but it will not take a day off my life. Thanks so much for sending me to that wonderful man." She checked her watch. "Goodness, it's getting late. I need to hurry home so I can tell Ollie the good news."

She fluttered out of the office like a bird liberated from a cage, leaving Christine and me to stare out the window as she flew to her Buick and gunned it out of the parking lot.

I turned to Christine. "Did you hear what she told me?"

Christine collapsed in an empty waiting-room chair. "Yes, I listened outside in the hallway. Isn't she just too much?" Then she let her head fall back against the wall as she exploded with laughter, shaking all over, tears coursing down her cheeks.

I found a chair across the room, laughing hysterically at the weird situation as well as at Christine's enjoyment of the situation. Finally, I regained my composure. "Tell me one thing. Did you know what she was going to say to me?"

She wiped the tears from her cheeks with a tissue. "Cross my heart. I thought she was mad at you. I'm as shocked as you are."

"Well, let's get out of here. My family's waiting for me, and no doubt you have better things to do. I guess Connie is happy because she has a diagnosis to tell to all her friends so they'll believe she really is sick. I'm surprised Dr. Lofton said that. He must have been frustrated to have made that comment."

Christine nodded in agreement. "What surprises me even more is that she latched on to it and thanked you for sending her to see him."

"Absolutely. People never cease to amaze me."

Chapter 23:

Traveling Sideshow

"**E**asy, Doc. That really hurts." Lonnie flinched, gasping as I gently palpated the wound. The incision in the lower back gapped open at least a centimeter, with the underlying tissue exposed, raw, and mildly inflamed. The vertical incision following lumbar laminectomy and disc excision had definitely not healed well. Several Steri-Strips at the bottom of the wound hung loosely, only partially attached on one side.

"Sorry, Lonnie, but I need to remove several of the Steri-Strips, cleanse the wound, and put on new Steri-Strips to hold the wound together. This is going to require close follow-up. When did you say you were returning home?"

Lonnie Jones was from Columbus, Ohio, and was visiting relatives in Glen Falls. His surgical wound had dehisced, and he found my office by calling the hospital switchboard for a list of local physicians. A friend had driven him to the office without calling ahead. Donna took him to the break area, examined the wound, and reported that he indeed needed attention. We included him on the schedule as a walk-in due to the urgency of the situation.

"How long ago did you say the surgery was done?"

"Two weeks ago."

"Did your surgeon tell you that it would be okay to travel this soon?"

Lonnie smiled and looked down. "Of course not. It's all my

fault. He said to rest at home for four weeks."

"Who did you say did your surgery?"

"Dr. Blackstone in Columbus, Ohio. He's an orthopedist but specializes in back surgeries."

"Exactly what did he do?"

"I was afraid you'd ask me that. I can never remember the big words used by doctors, so I brought my X-ray report for you to see." Lonnie pulled a crumpled, water-stained paper from his shirt pocket, worn around the edges with an irregular tear across the top of the page. He smiled at me as he placed it in my hands. "I accidentally tore the top off when it got wet in the rain a few days ago."

It was indeed an official-appearing report by a radiologist on the staff of a hospital in Columbus, Ohio. Unfortunately, the identifying information, including the patient's name and the date, had been torn off. Somewhere in the back of my mind, a red light briefly flashed on and off, but in the 1970s, there weren't many drug-seeking patients. Besides, I had been trained to give patients the benefit of the doubt. A doctor who didn't believe anything his patients told him would have great difficulty ever helping anyone. A basic level of trust is necessary in the doctor-patient relationship.

I looked up from the report at the friendly young man before me, neatly dressed, well groomed, in apparent pain with any significant movement of the back, and put the flashing red light out of my mind. "Very well, then, but you really should have your doctor run off another copy of your report. A description of the surgical procedure would also be helpful."

Lonnie nodded. "I plan to do just that, as soon as I get back home. But I need help getting back home. I'm out of pain pills, and my Ohio doctor doesn't have a license to prescribe them in Indiana. We stayed longer than I expected, so I didn't have enough. We'll be staying at least another week, so can you tide me over for at least a couple of weeks?" He looked hopefully at me, smiling and exuding charm. "Until I can get back to my doctor?"

It seemed an innocent-enough request, so Donna helped me cleanse the wound and reapply Steri-Strips while Lonnie held on to the examination table with a death grip. Finally finished, I asked, "What did you say you're were taking for pain?"

"I've been taking Dilaudid 4 mg four times daily. He gave me Tylenol #3 first, but it didn't stop the pain at all."

I frowned. "That's pretty strong."

Lonnie had an innocent baby face, which he turned imploringly to me. Feeling a twinge of guilt for doubting him, I said, "Tell you what. I'll write Dilaudid but only 2 mg four times daily for two weeks. That's fifty-six tablets to get you back home."

Lonnie looked disappointed. "Well, whatever you can do. I appreciate it."

Lonnie Jones was soon on his way and no longer in my thoughts as I finished my day in the office.

***

A week later, Donna placed twenty-six-year-old Mary McKnight in a room while I finished charts in the lab. Soon she placed Mary's chart in front of me. "I don't know about this one. Something doesn't strike me right."

I picked up the chart. "Is this a new patient?"

"Yes. New and temporary. She's visiting in Glen Falls with relatives this summer. She says that she's from Kansas."

"You don't believe her?"

"I don't know what to believe. Call it women's intuition, but something's not right. And she's out of her Dilaudid for chronic pain."

"Did she say why she has chronic pain?"

"Oh yes. And she has something to show you. I'll not ruin the surprise before you go see her."

I made my way to exam room 3 where Mary Smith awaited me. Dilaudid again. I wondered if there could be a connection to our patient of last week. My only patients on Dilaudid had terminal cancer.

In the room, I shook her hand, introducing myself and noting her appearance. Well dressed in a modest green suit, pearl necklace draped about her neck, deep blue eyes, and long auburn hair flowing about a somewhat plain but friendly face.

"Doctor, thank you so much for seeing me today. I'm very

grateful that you allowed me an appointment on such short notice."

"Quite all right. What seems to be the trouble, Miss McKnight?"

Batting her eyes and smiling, she said, "Please call me Mary."

"Okay, Mary it is. How can I help you today?"

"Did your lovely nurse tell you about my chronic pain?"

"A little. Can you be specific about your problem? I need a little background."

"Of course. About a year ago, I was injured in a terrible automobile accident. I was lucky to survive. I was driving with my window partially down when I was hit by another car. The left side of my head slammed into the driver's side window, breaking the glass and scraping off skin while I sustained injuries to my head and left ear. I was unconscious for several minutes. The medics took me to the hospital where I spent a week recovering. The surgeon had to operate on my severely damaged left ear." She swept the hair back to uncover her left ear. "You can see what happened."

Startled, I gazed open-mouthed at the healed wound. The lower half of her left ear was gone. It had been neatly excised just below the auditory canal. The upper ear was relatively undamaged. Everything had healed, but with irreversible damage very apparent. "That's quite a wound."

She looked sad. "It's something I have to live with the rest of my life."

I nodded. It was apparent why she wore her hair over her ears. I was still lost in thought as she went on explaining.

"So you see why I needed to see you today."

"What's that? Oh yes. Donna said you were in pain."

"Very much so. You see, I had a lot of nerve damage. Fortunately, I just have pain and not facial paralysis. The surgeon said I had a very close call."

"You could not have missed the facial nerve by much. That's for sure."

"My doctor has me on Dilaudid 4 mg every four hours as needed. I usually have to take at least four tablets a day."

I must have given her a skeptical look, because she immediately added, "Oh, I know I shouldn't. They are so habit forming." Her face brightened. "But my doctor is going to help me get off them when I get back home in a couple of weeks. I'm going to taper off and try something milder."

"I suppose I can prescribe a few for you to get back home, but no more than four tablets a day."

I picked up my pen and prescription pad but hesitated. She smiled beautifully, brushed her hair back once more, and began gently massaging the remnants of her left ear, flinching from time to time.

Oh, well. I knew I'd never figure this out in one visit. I quickly filled out the prescription for Dilaudid 4 mg four times daily as needed, scribbled my name at the bottom, and handed it to her.

She glanced at her prescription. "Only fifty-six tablets?"

"Yes. If your own doctor in Kansas wants you to have more, that will be up to him."

She stuck out her hand. "Thanks for what you've done for me. I'll make them last."

I met Donna in the hallway after she had placed another patient in a room. "Well, what did you think of her?"

"I'm not sure. There's no denying the ear trauma. Still, she didn't seem in as much pain as she claimed."

Donna smiled. "Let me guess. You gave her a prescription anyway."

"I guess I'm a softy, but I'll give almost anyone the benefit of the doubt as least once. We'll probably never know if I was right to give her the prescription or not."

Donna glanced down at the charts in her hand. "I can't help but wonder." She raised her eyes to look up at me. "That may not be the last we hear from her."

"Woman's intuition?"

She nodded emphatically. "Woman's intuition."

Mary Smith was soon forgotten with the pressure of high-patient volume. At last, the day drew to an end, and we locked up for the night.

***

Ten days later, I entered the lab/break room to work on a couple of charts, only to find Christine waiting for me. "Dr. Matlock, I have a patient on hold wanting an appointment, but I need to clear this with you first. Donna said I should."

"Sure. What's the problem?"

"Another out-of-state patient is out of pain medicine. Should we see him or not?"

"I don't know. We do seem to be getting a run on patients out of their narcotics. What's the complaint this time?"

Christine rolled her eyes. "A young man named John Brown, supposedly. He's post-op brain surgery and needs medicine until he gets back to his own doctor in Ohio."

I shrugged. "Do we even have any open spots this afternoon?"

"A couple. What do you want me to tell him?"

"It shouldn't be difficult to see if he really has had recent brain surgery. I guess it's okay since we aren't full this afternoon. I hate to say no if he's legitimate. We've not had a problem with drug addiction in the past—that is, unless these 'out-of-state' people are lying."

Christine breezed out of the lab. "I'll put him on for the last appointment today."

Donna entered the lab with the chart for the next patient. "So you're going to let John Brown in today?"

"I don't see a good reason not to see him since we have open slots."

She shook her head and frowned. "You're the boss."

"Do you know something that I don't know?"

She smiled. "Woman's intuition, Doc. Just that. Nothing more."

Nothing else was said until the end of the day when Donna handed me the last chart. "Here's your last one for the day, Mr. John Brown. And I still say 'woman's intuition.'"

"Okay, Miss Sherlock Holmes. You may well be right, but we won't have to put up with out-of-state patients for long. What does he want?"

"Need you ask?"

"Dilaudid?"

Donna laughed. "You may collect your prize money. You guessed right the first time."

Within a short time, I was seated in the exam room 2 with John Brown as he spun his tale of woe. His head was shaved. There was a long but well-healed incision on the left side from the occipital area, or back of the head, extending to just above his upper forehead. His eyes looked vacant as they shifted dully around the room.

With his speech mildly slurred, he began, "Ya see, it's this way, Doc. I had a bike wreck on my Harley. Lost control on a curve. Ended up sliding down the pavement on my head. Got knocked out and woke up in the hospital. Lucky to be alive. My head swathed in bandages. Couldn't think straight for a week. Severe migraines ever since."

"How long ago did this happen?"

"Ten, twelve weeks ago, maybe? My memory's not good after that bump on the noggin."

"Tell me about the pain. On a scale of one to ten, with ten being the worst and one the least, how much pain are you having?"

"Yeah, the pain. Severe. Twenty out of ten. Indescribable really." John Brown appeared to be out of energy. He hung his head, staring dully at the floor, waiting on my response.

"Let's have a look at you, Mr. Brown."

I did a thorough examination, including a detailed neurologic evaluation. The only positive findings besides slurred speech were mild hyporeflexia, or diminished reflexes in all extremities, and mild ataxic gait. He was unable to walk in tandem or stand with his feet together. There was also a distinct odor of alcohol on his breath.

"What medicine did you say you are taking for pain?"

He perked up at that question. "Dilaudid 4 mg every four hours around the clock."

"Really?"

"Yeah. I hurt really bad. Need my medicine. Enough for three or four weeks until I get back home."

"Who did you say you doctor with?"

"Dr. Green's my family doctor. He's in charge of my medicine now. The surgeon released me from care."

I stood and picked up his chart. "Give me a few minutes. I'll be back soon."

Christine stood at the end of the hallway where she could not be seen by patients in the waiting room. She motioned me down the hall to the break room, quickly entering and closing the door behind her as I made my way there. She and Christine huddled, whispering to one another, when I joined them.

"What's up, ladies?"

Donna smiled knowingly and motioned Christine to proceed.

"Mary McKnight just walked in. She's in the waiting room, claiming she lost her prescription, 'spilled down the sink,' don't you know? She needs a new prescription to replace it."

"That's not the best part," Donna chimed in. "Guess who's waiting in the car for her."

Feeling weary now, I sighed. "I'm not sure, but I'm sure you're going to tell me."

Donna smiled triumphantly. "Lonnie Johnson. He has on dark sunglasses, but I'm sure it's him."

"We're pretty sure they dropped John Brown off and drove down the street, only returning a few minutes later," Christine added. "We think all three of them are together."

"It looks like you were right, Donna."

"That's not all," Christine said. "Dr. Green is supposed to call right back. We talked with his office. He wants to speak with you."

As if in fulfillment of prophecy, the phone rang, and Christine picked up the receiver in the lab area. She quickly motioned me to the phone. Handing me the phone, she whispered, "We noticed that both Lonnie Johnson and John Brown listed Dr. Green in Columbus as the family doctor. So we called him." (In those days, privacy concerns were not paramount. There was nothing illegal about checking on patients regarding possible abuse. The day when internet searches of patients and their prescription purchases awaited the future.)

"Hello, Dr. Green. This is Dr. Matlock in Glen Oaks, Indiana. I have two patients here who claim that you are their family doctor. They also said that you have been prescribing Dilaudid for chronic pain for them." I went on to describe Lonnie Jones and John

Brown and their requests. "At least, that's the stories they gave here in the office over the last few days."

Dr. Green's booming voice came over the receiver. "I find this all very interesting, Dr. Matlock. They got Dilaudid from me by telling me you were their doctor and had prescribed it. They claimed to be visiting here from Indiana. I believe we've both been hoodwinked. It's very interesting that they have prominent wounds to demonstrate in order to obtain Dilaudid. I'll give odds that we're not the only ones they're calling on."

"Thanks for taking time to call back, Dr. Green. This crew is probably selling most of the Dilaudid and getting high on the rest. I'll notify the doctors in my area at the county medical society meeting later this week. They must be following the interstate east-west routes between Indiana and Ohio, hitting up physicians all along the way."

"Thanks. I'll do the same here. Maybe we can help put a stop to their phony gambit. I'll also notify the Ohio State Police. Perhaps you can do the same in Indiana with your state police."

"I'll do it, and thanks again."

After hanging up, I filled in the ladies on the conversation. "Now we have to find a safe way to get them out of the office. I hope they don't have any weapons on them."

Christine folded her arms across her chest and assumed a smug look. "We already thought of that."

"And?"

"That wonderful Marty Blackwell is on police duty this afternoon. He should be here any time now. You can relax." She offered me my cup. "Here, have another cup of coffee while we wait."

Within mere moments, we heard the front door open and Donna cracked the lab door to peer out. "He's here. Come on, Christine. Let's go talk to him while Doc empties out the office."

As I followed the ladies from the lab, I noticed Mary McKnight edging toward the outside door. I hurried down the hall, not wanting John Brown to miss his ride. Flinging the door open, I found him going through the drawers and in the process of stuffing my prescription pad into his pants pocket. "Why, Mr. Brown. I believe you're making a mistake. That pad of paper belongs to me."

He looked down at his hands, hesitated, and then pulled the pad back out of his pocket before laying it on my small desktop. "Guess you're right. Must be my brain injury actin' up again. Not thinkin' too clear. How about my prescription?"

"About that. I just talked with Dr. Green in Columbus, Ohio. Need I say more?"

His face flushed and he reached for the prescription pad again. Apparently his "brain damage" was not severe enough to shield him from the implications of that call.

John Brown was a big man, at least six feet two inches tall and probably two-hundred fifty pounds. But I had an edge. I laid my hand on the prescription pad and said, "Come with me and meet my friend, Martin Blackwell, our town police officer. He's in the waiting room now."

"Huh? What? I didn't do nothin'."

"Not yet anyway. Come along. Leave quietly and I'll not press charges."

Muttering under his breath, John Brown, or whoever he was, swayed unsteadily down the hallway to the waiting room. He eyed the blue uniform and the muscular man wearing it before heading toward the exit door.

Marty Blackwell stood tall, smiling at the ladies, grinning from ear to ear. "Need any help, Doc?"

"Not right now, but you might want to get the license number of that car waiting on him."

He pulled out his writing pad. "They with him?"

"I believe so. Let's watch what happens."

The late-model Ford had pulled nearly to the street, but the plates identifying the vehicle were easily readable. John Brown stumbled across the parking lot, yanked open the door, and nearly fell getting into the back seat. As he reached out to close the door, the driver tromped on the gas pedal and roared out of the lot and down the street.

Marty Blackwell laughed. "That was priceless. Best entertainment I've had all day. I got the plate number and auto description. I'll call it in to the sheriff's department and Indiana State Police. I don't think we have anything to arrest them on, do we?"

"They didn't steal anything but our time, if that's what you mean. But they are hitting up doctors for drugs, falsifying records."

"I'll get this out right away. If they're stopped for any reason, we might be able to catch them with the goods."

"Thanks for coming so quick, Marty."

"Yes, thanks," the ladies chimed in. "We appreciate you."

"Glad to do it." Marty winked at the ladies and went back to his car to radio his report, obviously putting out a bulletin on the trio that had just departed.

"I was sure relieved to see him. Our John Brown thought about stealing a prescription pad, right in front of me."

Christine had a dreamy look on her face. "We were glad to see Marty too. Weren't we, Donna?"

"Yes, I certainly agree, but I think you had ulterior motives."

I laughed at the continuing banter between the ladies as I locked the front door and returned to the back to finish my charts.

***

Two days later, I arrived at the office to begin the day with news for the staff. Finding them in the break room, I announced, "You'll be interested in what I found out last night at the county medical society meeting."

"What's the news?" Christine piped up.

"You no doubt remember the trio Marty Blackwell helped chase out of here."

They nodded, smiling.

"It seems that at least five other doctors were taken by them. So I don't feel quite so bad for being fooled."

"Their wounds looked real enough," Donna said. "I don't doubt that sometime in the past every one of them sustained an injury or surgical wound."

"I agree. The amazing thing is that the one who called himself Lonnie Jones had to be keeping the wound on his back open for display. He had a low-grade infection in the wound. He may pay a serious price for his masquerade, if that worsens and spreads through his body. We haven't had much substance abuse in this community in the past. I guess that's why several of the doctors, myself included, were taken in by their clever scheme. I for one will try to be more careful in the future. I just hope this isn't a trend in our country. Those young people are going to destroy their lives."

The trio of pretenders did not return to our office, but I still wonder what happened to them. I hope they got the help they really needed.

Chapter 24:

Cardiac Arrest

"Code blue, emergency room. Code blue, emergency room."

I had just flipped on the light beside my name announcing my presence when the loud clanging of the alarm sounded for several seconds, followed by the repeated summons for emergency rescuers over the PA system. I glanced at my watch—6:45 a.m.—and sprinted for the ER.

I had a bad feeling about this one. Jenny Whitcomb, a pleasant, elderly patient had called me at home before I left for hospital rounds, advising that the ambulance had arrived for her husband, Harvey Whitcomb. He was experiencing crushing chest pain and sweating. I had promised to meet them in the ER that morning.

Since the ER was nearly a block down the hall from the doctors' entrance, I arrived winded but anxious to learn the identity of the cardiac-arrest patient. Ann Kilgore pointed to trauma room 1 and mouthed Harvey's name. Trauma 1, our largest ER room, was used for both medical and trauma codes.

I ran to the room, then recovered my breath while taking in the details. Dr. John Neal, a highly competent ER physician, was running the code from the head of the bed. The monitor showed ventricular fibrillation, a disorganized quivering of the lower chambers of the heart without any effective pumping action of blood so necessary to sustain life.

The bed was surrounded by assistants engaged in the rescue effort. I had difficulty seeing the patient for all the emergency helpers, until Dr. Neal saw me standing inside the doorway and motioned me to join him at the head of the bed.

"Hey, Carl. Do you know the story on this gentleman?" he asked. "His wife is hysterical and couldn't tell me much. He arrested right after we got him in here." He nodded toward the monitor. "You can see what we have now."

I looked up at the chaotic, disorganized rhythm of ventricular fibrillation and nodded. "Harvey is a mild diabetic with hypertension. His diabetes is diet controlled and his blood pressure has been easily managed with a diuretic. I think I have him on hydrochlorothiazide 50 mg daily. I'll have to check my records to be sure, but he's been well controlled. Blood pressure usually about 145/85. No previous cardiac events that I know about. He recently turned seventy-one and came in for a general checkup. No real complaints at the time."

I watched the rescue effort as our conversation continued. Dr. Neal had intubated Harvey with a size 8 ET (endotracheal tube) in the trachea. One ER nurse was bagging (ventilating) him with a hand-operated bag-valve combination connected to the ET tube at about twelve breaths per minute. The respiratory bag-valve device had oxygen being delivered through a long tube at 10 liters per minute via connection with the wall outlet valve marked *Oxygen*. The respiratory therapist had not arrived, as an ICU patient on a mechanical ventilator had decompensated, requiring her attention.

The EMTs were taking turns doing compressions over the sternum (breastbone) as Dr. Neal monitored the pulse in the left carotid artery with his left index and middle fingers, gently palpating the artery to gauge the effectiveness of the effort. One ER nurse was taping an IV of normal saline in place in Harvey's left antecubital fossa (the inner side of the elbow joint). A medicine floor nurse was busy trying to get a second IV in the right forearm. A third nurse from the surgical floor was keeping a record of medications given along with the time of administration, while Ann Kilgore stood by the crash cart ready to hand any meds needed to the two nurses managing the IVs.

Dr. Neal turned to me. "Here's the story. Your patient was

talking to the EMTs as they pulled into the hospital driveway from Main Street. He had complained of severe chest pain for about an hour at that time. He developed a bradycardic rate of about thirty. Unfortunately, the monitor or leads malfunctioned about that time and we have no actual record of the bradycardic rhythm. They quickly put it right, but by then he had developed PVCs (premature ventricular contractions), followed by runs of VT (ventricular tachycardia – a rapid and usually unstable rhythm), then V-fib (ventricular fibrillation). I tried an immediate chest thump as we wheeled him into the room. No response to that, and we shocked him twice just before you arrived. I gave him 1 mg of epinephrine through the IV on the left and was trying to get a second IV started. We are getting a fair pulse with CPR. I was about ready to shock him again."

"Sounds like you're on top of it. Go ahead with the shock."

By then, both IVs were taped in place. Dr. Neal surveyed the code effort, which continued as an ER nurse charged the defibrillator to 360 joules. She nodded at Dr. Neal, and he announced, "All clear." Everyone stood back from the metal cart while the nurse applied the paddles to Harvey's chest and repeated the warning. Dr. Neal glanced at the position of all rescuers, making sure no one else would be shocked, then said, "Okay. Deliver shock."

Harvey's body jerked forcefully on the cart when the current was applied. Dr. Neal nodded, and the EMTs got ready to resume chest compressions.

I anxiously watched the monitor, and seeing favorable blips, said, "Hold on a minute. I believe we have a normal sinus rhythm."

Dr. Neal smiled. "We do indeed. See if you can get a blood pressure. I'm feeling a faint pulse in the carotid artery."

Ann quickly confirmed that we had a BP of 95/68 in the right forearm. Harvey's color rapidly improved as his BP quickly rose to 128/75.

I turned to Dr. Neal. "Great job. Now we'll get him to ICU." I looked at Ann. "I hope we have an ICU bed."

Ann was at the end of a night shift as supervisor. "We have three empty beds, Doc. No problem. The Whitcombs are my neighbors. I'll help you get him settled. I want to see about Jenny before I go home."

I accompanied Ann, the EMTs, and two nurses to the ICU with Harvey on the ER cart. Holly, the respiratory therapist, had arrived and was assisting with transport, bagging him while we rolled the cart along. The ER monitor sounded a reassuring regular *beep* with each heartbeat.

"Doc, he's starting to breathe on his own. I'm just going to assist him now. He seems to be waking up a little."

"Great. That's encouraging. Be sure his hands are restrained. I don't want him pulling out his ET tube or IV as he's waking up."

After arriving in ICU, we transferred Harvey to a regular bed and switched over to an ICU monitor. He began making purposeful movements with his hands and legs, so the nurses tied his hands to the bedrails with padded arm restraints to prevent accidental dislodgement of his airway, IVs, or cardiac monitor leads.

Ann stood beside the bed for a minute, checking on vital signs so she could relate them to Jenny, then retrieved the ER monitor from the end of the bed, placed it on the ER cart, and started rolling the cart to the ICU double doors. "See you later. I'll let Jenny know what's going on before I go home to get some sleep. I'll have one of the aides bring her up on the elevator to the ICU waiting room where you can talk with her later."

"Thanks for your help. It's always appreciated." I glanced up at the monitor as the doors swung shut behind Ann. The beeping had become irregular, and I noted multiple PVCs.

Linda Ottinger, head nurse of ICU, noticed the irregular rhythm and hurried to join me at the bedside. "It looks like he's developing an unstable rhythm again."

"He sure is. Draw up 100 mg of lidocaine and give it IV push ASAP. Then please get a liter of D5W with lidocaine mix and start a continuous drip of lidocaine at 2 mg per minute, titrating up to 4 mg

---

[3] Some of the medications, such as lidocaine, are rarely used during treatment of acute myocardial infarction today. Medicine is in a constant state of flux with new drugs, new therapies, and new procedures as knowledge of the human body is constantly advancing. That is the challenge of medicine today: just trying to stay current.

per minute if needed to suppress the PVCs."[3]

"We're on it, Doc. Liz, grab a vial of lidocaine and draw up 100 mg to give IV push stat."

Liz O'Conner sprang from her seat at the nurses station, where she had been charting and watching the monitors, and ran to the emergency medicine cart. "Be right there."

Before we could get the lidocaine started, Harvey stiffened all over, then developed brief seizure-like activity as the alarms on the monitor sounded off and the beeping blurred into a continuous loud warning-mode sound.

A quick look at the monitor showed V-fib and Harvey had no pulse again. As his body relaxed, I pulled up his eyelids and noted dilated, poorly reactive pupils. "Start CPR."

Liz injected the lidocaine while an aide gave the code-blue alert to the switchboard. Linda was already doing chest compressions, and Holly ran to the bed to begin bagging again.

"Liz, get the defibrillator over here quick and charge to three hundred sixty joules. We'll shock him as soon as possible." She rushed to carry out the orders as the ICU doors crashed open to admit a small army of willing assistants. If prolonged, CPR is physically and emotionally draining.

We were one minute into the code when Liz said, "Ready with shock at 360."

"Okay. Everybody clear," I said. Pausing to allow Holly to lay the ventilator bag on the bed, I looked once more to ensure safety for all the participants. "Apply shock now."

Liz pressed the buttons on the paddles she held on his chest and said, "Shock delivered," as his muscles once again contracted from the shock, resulting in a quick jerking of the body. Meanwhile, Linda had grabbed the large resuscitation board to place beneath Harvey, as it would allow firmer compressions than we could obtain with him lying on the bed mattress. With helping hands, he was quickly log-rolled onto his right side as the board was slid beneath him. Then he was log-rolled back and centered on the board for CPR to continue.

Liz stepped up to take a turn at chest compressions and positioned her hands over the sternum to begin. Looking up at the monitor, she froze in place as steady beeping resumed. Normal P waves followed by QRS complexes repetitively marched across the screen, indicating normal conduction in the heart once more. A quick check confirmed a steady pulse with BP of 100/63. I raised first the right upper eyelid, then the left, and noted that the pupils had returned to a smaller, mid-position size and were fully reactive, constricting when I shined my pocket light into the eyes.

Harvey began to stir, moaning softly, so we retied the hand restraints that had been removed during CPR to prevent contact with the bed frame during cardioversion. I could smell singed chest hair from the latest shock. The last thing he needed was burns of his hands or wrists.

Harvey continued to wake up over the next several minutes, so I sat down and wrote orders for his care. Just as I finished, Linda Ottinger handed me the first EKG we had been able to get. "Doesn't look too good."

"No, it doesn't. A big anterior MI (myocardial infarction or heart attack) with ST elevation extending from V1 to V5. I don't like the looks of it. I'm going to the ICU waiting room to talk with his wife, Jenny. He may not do well. The EMTs reported some type of bradycardic rhythm just before he arrested the first time. Keep the lidocaine going and turn it up to 4 mg per minute. Monitor his blood pressure every fifteen minutes for now. The lidocaine might drop his pressure, but he needs it to stabilize his rhythm now."

"Are we going to keep him here for treatment?"

"I don't know yet. He could end up needing an emergency pacemaker. I'm suspicious of serious ischemia involving the septal cardiac conduction system with the history of bradycardia preceding V-fib. I wish we had a good tracing of the bradycardic event, but some of the leads either came loose in the ambulance or the monitor malfunctioned briefly. The EMTs were sure the pulse was down in the low thirties, but when they got the leads repositioned, he developed multiple PVCs followed by V-tach and V-fib. We have no definite record immediately documenting the type of bradycardia that seemed to initiate the ventricular arrhythmias and cardiac arrest."

I left the ICU to find Jenny Whitcomb, whom I urgently needed to talk with about the prognosis and treatment. I found her in the ICU waiting room with Ann Kilgore, who still had not gone home to rest.

"I decided to stay with Jenny until her daughter gets here from Indianapolis," Ann said. "Her son lives in Illinois, so she doesn't have anyone else to be with her at the moment."

Jenny reached over and patted Ann's hand. "She's a good neighbor and friend, but please tell me, how is my Harvey doing? What are his chances?"

No other families were in the waiting room, so I pulled up a chair opposite Jenny. "Harvey is beginning to wake up now. Unfortunately, he required defibrillation, meaning electrical shocks, three times already, twice in the ER and once here. The EMTs documented a very slow pulse. That's what we call bradycardia. Unfortunately, they had trouble with the monitor or the electrical leads and couldn't document the slow rhythm. Whatever type bradycardia it was, and there are different types, it preceded the first cardiac arrest by about thirty or forty seconds. By the time they had the monitor working again, he was having problems with rapid heartbeats, called tachycardia. He has been very unstable since then and is in critical condition."

Jenny began to tear up again, quickly dabbing her handkerchief over her eyes and cheeks.

"Now don't give up hope. He is waking up, and that's a good sign. He appears more stable, but time will tell. What I'm worried about is the extent of the heart damage. The EKG looks like a large anterior myocardial infarction. Those words probably don't mean much to you, but what that means is that a large part of the anterior, or frontal, aspect of the ventricles is affected. The ventricles receive blood from the upper small atrial chambers, but the ventricles are the main pumping chambers. If too much damage occurs to the ventricles, that can lead to congestive heart failure, shock, or serious rhythm problems if the conduction system is damaged as well. In other words, if any of these more serious problems develop, I'll need to transfer him to an Indianapolis hospital."

Jenny shuddered and began to weep, stifling sobs with her handkerchief.

Ann slipped her arm around her. "You just take care of Harvey. I'll stay here with Jenny until some of her family arrives. We know you'll take good care of Harvey."

Jenny wiped her eyes again, blew her nose, and nodded in agreement. "Yes, just please take good care of him. I don't know how I'd live without him."

That was the beginning of a long day for me and for Harvey and his family. I had no sooner re-entered ICU, than his monitor again went off. A quick glance revealed recurrent V-fib. Since everything was still at the bedside, I simply recharged the defibrillator and applied the pads to his chest while Linda called a code and Liz hurried to help me. Harvey was unconscious again.

"Everyone clear." I glanced about, then quickly said, "Stay clear. Applying shock," and pressed the button. Once more, Harvey jerked, but rapidly regained consciousness as his heart resumed beating.

"How are you, Harvey?" I asked.

He looked up and mumbled, "Okay, I think."

Dr. Bill Johnson joined me at the bedside, along with a half dozen others responding to the code. He laughed and shook his head. "This becoming a habit with you? Enjoying the excitement of code-blue exercises?"

"It looks like it." I proceeded to give him a quick history as he stood nodding, taking it in. Dr. Johnson was a highly experienced older family doctor whose advice I valued. He had much experience in reading EKGs and in administering general anesthesia at our hospital as well.

As we talked, the monitor again sounded. Glancing up, I saw what I dreaded most, complete heart block. Normally the pacemaker in the upper right chamber (right atrium) sets the pace and rhythm of the heart. The heart attack had interrupted that by blocking the connection between the sinus node pacemaker and the ventricular AV pacemaker (atrioventricular node, a secondary pacemaker). Although the sinus node pacemaker in the atrium was working and attempting to send a signal to the AV node to set the pace, the AV node had completely ceased to function. No signals were being accepted. The only electrical stimulus for the ventricles to beat came from a ventricular escape pacemaker, well below the AV node, and firing at about twenty-eight beats per minute. I had been right in guessing ischemia, poor perfusion of the conduction system.

We had no cardiologist on staff other than consulting cardiologists who came only when called for in-hospital consultations. Whatever was done, I would have to do it. I had been fortunate to spend three months working with cardiologists reading EKGs and attending cardiology conferences during training. More importantly, I had worked a fourth month assisting in cardiac cath lab and had put in several right-heart pacemakers during procedures that might result in the need for temporary pacing. That had all been done under Dr. Hill's supervision while using fluoroscopy for placement of the pacemaker. Now a pacemaker would have to be floated in "blind," for we had no way to do fluoroscopy this time.

Harvey was still conscious, barely. With my right hand, I grasped Dr. Johnson's left wrist. "Will you help me? He needs a pacemaker right now. I've put in several temporary pacemakers with fluoroscopy while working with cardiologist Alan Hill during my training. I know you've put in some emergency pacemakers as well."

"Sure thing, Carl. Let's get started."

Linda stood on the other side of the bed ready to assist. "What do you need?"

"We haven't put any of these in for a year or more, but we should have an emergency temporary pacemaker pack in stock," Dr. Johnson said.

Linda stared up at the ceiling for a few seconds, then glanced over at us. "I know where it's at." She then called out, "Liz, look on the top shelf of the supply cupboard just off our break room. There should be a box with a sterile pacemaker set located there. It should be prominently labeled."

Dr. Johnson headed for the EKG machine. "We'll float this in by setting up an electrode with an EKG. Go ahead and get prepped while I set this up."

Liz prepped Harvey's right upper arm with a sterile sponge and Hibiclens surgical soap while I scrubbed in preparation for the procedure. Linda went to the ICU waiting room to explain the placement of a temporary pacemaker to Jenny and have a consent form signed. Mrs. Whitcomb had only had one brief chance to see him so far, so after signing the form, Linda and Ann brought her back. She stood at the foot of the bed between both nurses while we set up. Harvey seemed to smile at her before they took her back out.

The leads for an EKG were all in place, and Dr. Johnson unhooked the V1 right chest lead to use as an exploring electrode during continuous EKG monitoring. While he set that up, I put on a sterile gown, surgical cap, gloves, and mask. He wheeled a procedure tray over to the bedside, placed the temporary pacemaker set on it, and peeled off the cover. I was then able to reach inside the sterile set and remove the pacemaker with accompanying catheter sheath for placement.

After spreading sterile towels over the area and leaving the right upper arm exposed, I cannulated the right brachial vein with the needle and catheter set, then threaded the pacemaker wire inside the catheter sheath up through the axillary and subclavian veins. Dr. Johnson hooked the V1 lead on the non-sterile end of the pacemaker wire that I handed him. Immediately, we could see the configuration of the EKG change on the V1 lead as I carefully advanced it through the superior vena cava, into the right atrium, and finally into the right ventricle. I had been lucky in quick placement. That was not the usual situation.

He nodded encouragement. "Now all you have to do is anchor it in the wall of the right ventricle. Advance the catheter wire carefully while I help you watch for the right QRS form to appear."

I very carefully inched the pacemaker wire forward into the right ventricle, sweating all the while. Harvey was having short runs of V-tach again. The pacemaker wire itself could set off arrhythmias until we had it properly functioning. I held my breath as the QRS complex changed in V1 as I progressed toward the ventricular wall.

"Bingo!" Dr. Johnson yelled out. "You got it. Now to hook it up." He quickly removed the V1 lead and attached the temporary pacemaker unit in its place, switched it on, adjusted the sensitivity, and set a rate of seventy beats per minute. A beautiful smile wreathed his face as he said, "Just look at that. Perfect capture."

As I removed my cap, gown, and gloves, the nurses placed a sterile dressing over the cannulated vein.

Harvey was waking up, considerably more alert. He grinned at me. "Hi, Doc. How are you? You don't know how good it is to see you. I think I had a heart attack."

***

A chest X-ray confirmed placement, a fact we had confirmed with the EKG pattern already. More importantly, there was no sign of congestive heart failure. He did have mild cardiac enlargement, consistent with longstanding hypertension.

Ann brought Jenny back in the ICU to see her husband. It was a good time for me to speak with them together, so I stepped to the foot of the bed where Jenny was seated on Harvey's left, beside an IV pole. As they looked up expectantly, I said, "Harvey, you've had a close call. Dr. Johnson assisted me in getting a temporary transvenous pacemaker placed in your heart. Your normal pacemakers weren't working to control your heart rate and rhythm. You've had a significant heart attack that has at least temporarily damaged your own natural pacemakers. They may start to function again, or they may not. When your heart rate dropped down to twenty-eight to thirty beats per minute, we had no time to waste. Jenny gave consent for a pacemaker, and now you have one."

Harvey asked, "Is twenty-eight to thirty too slow?"

"I'll say it is. We have your pacemaker set at seventy right now. The problem is that this may be a permanent situation. You may very well require a permanent pacemaker, and we aren't set up to put in those kind in our county hospital here at Glen Falls."

Jenny looked distressed. "What are you trying to tell us? Does he need to have another surgery?"

"That's a good question, but I don't know the answer for sure. My guess is yes, he probably needs a permanent pacemaker in view of the damage to his heart's conduction system. It could be just temporary ischemia, meaning insufficient blood flow, but the odds are against that because of the EKG evidence of fairly extensive damage."

Harvey looked worried. "Do I have to go to another hospital? Is that what you're saying?"

"For your own safety, yes. If you consent, I'll place a call to my good friend Dr. Hill, an outstanding cardiologist in my books. He has a practice in Indianapolis and is on several hospital staffs. Knowing him, it's likely he'll want you transferred to Indiana University Medical Center and placed in University Hospital—that is, if an ICU bed is available. Is that okay with you?"

They glanced at one another, then Jenny answered for both. "We want what's best for Harvey. We greatly appreciate what you and Dr. Johnson did for us, and we trust you to make the right decisions."

Harvey looked me in the eye. "One more thing. You'll still be my primary care doctor, won't you?"

I smiled. "Of course. I often work with Dr. Hill. He has consulted and helped me care for a number of my patients."

At that, Harvey visibly relaxed. "Then it's okay with me."

***

I still had to make hospital rounds, and Donna and Christine had rearranged the schedule to accommodate our office patients. Most everyone knew Harvey Whitcomb. Since news travels fast in small towns, no one complained about the necessary changes in the appointments for the day.

In a short time, transfer was arranged and Harvey was on his way to Indiana University Hospital on the main medical center campus. Once there, further testing indeed revealed the need for a permanent pacemaker, which he had implanted without complications.

I'm happy to say that Harvey lived several years beyond the episode with the pacemaker.

Chapter 25:

Life-Threatening Syncope

"Doc, what's makin' me black out?"

Wilbur Harding, eighty-one-year-old patriarch of his clan, sat stroking the stubble of gray whiskers on his chin. His brown tweed suitcoat with slightly frayed sleeves had seen better days and presented a striking contrast with the faded blue bib-overalls and red-checkered flannel shirt. Down-at-the-heel gray cowboy boots completed his attire.

"That's what I'm trying to figure out, Mr. Harding. The medical record from the ER states that you took down sixty feet of your neighbor's fence and that you had no recollection of the accident." I glanced at the chart copy from our ER, noting a relatively normal EKG for a man his age, as well as CBC, electrolytes, and renal functions normal. Chest X-ray with mild cardiomegaly and minimal calcification of the aortic arch. Nothing really significant.

"It's not true that I don't remember. I was drivin' my '55 Ford pickup truck, haulin' feed for my cattle, about five thirty in the mornin'. Next thing I remember is wakin' up with my truck on its side in a muddy ditch. It's right in sayin' that I tore down about sixty feet of fence. That was Pete Gilroy's farm fence. I done paid him for it. So see, I do remember. There's nothin' wrong with my mind."

"I don't think that's what they mean. Of course your mind is okay, but you don't seem to know what made you crash in the first place, do you?"

"Well now, maybe I don't. But my mind's okay. Doc, that police officer threatened to take my driver's license. Said maybe I was drunk. So I took their fool alcohol test. It showed negative, just like I told 'em it would."

How to explain? "Wilbur, I know you are an intelligent, successful farmer. I'm not worried about your mind in the way you're referring to. What everyone is concerned about is that you don't remember what happened that caused you to wreck. The ER doctor said you were the only one on the road. No one else was involved in the accident. Isn't that correct?"

"Now that you put it that way, I suppose that's right. And for a fact, I don't remember what made me wreck my truck."

"Were you perhaps looking around while driving? Not paying close attention to where you were?"

A hurt look came into Wilbur's eyes. "Why, I never, never did no such a thing."

"I didn't ask that to offend you. Just trying to piece this together. It sounds like the ER doctor was correct in diagnosing you as 'syncope—unknown etiology.'"

"What's that 'syncope etiology' mean? Is that some kind of insult?"

"Not at all. It is just a fancy way of saying that you fainted but the cause remains unknown."

"Well, why didn't the young feller just say that?"

I chuckled. "Because he's a doctor. Like me, I guess. We often use words that sound mysterious, but they all have significant meaning."

"In other words, he's just a smarty pants."

I shook my head. "No. I don't mean that either. Dr. Neal is always very professional in his dealing with patients. He's really a very good ER doctor. I'm sure he just wanted to convey to me his concern that a better diagnosis be discovered before you get hurt."

"In other words, he's sayin' that he didn't know what happened."

"That's one way of putting it."

Wilbur slapped his knee and cackled. "He's not so smart. I don't know what happened, but neither does he. That makes us kind of even, don't it?"

I had to laugh along with him. "Okay, you got me there. Let's get you up on the examination table and take a look at you."

After I helped him step up on the stool and then onto the table where he sat on the side, Wilbur handed me his wooden cane. "Here, Doc. Put this somewhere."

"Can we slip off your suitcoat, unfasten your overall straps, and get you out of your shirt?"

"Sure can. But I'll need your help. My girl gave me this new shirt and it's a little too tight."

As I assisted him getting his tweed coat off, I mentally reviewed Donna's notes. *Occasionally dizzy, always very brief episodes. No chest pain or trouble breathing. Arises at 4:30 a.m. and goes to bed "with the chickens."* I'm sure those were his exact words she had in quotes. Donna enjoyed the quaint humor of our farmers.

After unbuttoning the lower buttons of his shirt, pulling it wide open to reveal a hairy chest, Wilbur reached up to unfasten the top button on his collar, tugged on it, and then reeled about on the cart. He emitted a brief moaning sound. "Oh, oh."

I grabbed him to prevent a fall from the table and yelled, "Donna, I need help! Hurry!"

The door burst open and both Donna and Christine rushed to my assistance. Wilbur was a big man, six feet four inches tall weighing in at 275 pounds. It took all three to turn him sideways, pull out the footrest, and lower him to a supine position on the table.

Christine stepped back and took a deep breath. "Whew. He's bigger than I thought. What in the world happened? Is he all right?"

Donna sprang into action, stooped over to check his blood pressure first. I whipped out my stethoscope to listen to his heart as Donna looked up in consternation. "His pulse! It's very slow and irregular."

I was just confirming that for myself with the stethoscope.

"Pulse around thirty-five and irregular. Quick, get the EKG. He's breathing, but slowly. We might have to do CPR."

"I'll get it for you." Christine opened the door and ran to the lab.

Within moments, Donna had the EKG plugged in with the leads all attached. Meanwhile, I continued to monitor his heart, holding the stethoscope with my left hand while flicking up his eyelids with my right index finger to check the pupils. They were normal. As Donna started the EKG recording, Wilbur swallowed and began to stir on the table.

I placed my right hand on his chest. "Don't move, Wilbur. We're checking an EKG."

Donna handed me the EKG, which showed a sinus bradycardia rhythm with a rate of thirty-nine. There was no sign of acute injury to the heart.

Wilbur now had his eyes open, looking directly at me. "I don't feel so good. Could I have a glass of water, please?"

Sighing in relief, I said, "I don't see why not. But just you stay still on the exam table for a minute until you're feeling better."

His pulse had picked up to fifty-five while his color improved. Still holding my fingers on his left radial pulse, I laid my stethoscope aside. "You gave us a scare. Were you having pain in your chest before you passed out?"

Wilbur shook his head. "No pain. And can I sit up now? I'm feelin' fine."

"Wait until Donna finishes checking your blood pressure one more time. Your pulse is back up to seventy-six now. That's much better."

Donna straightened up. "Blood pressure good. 145/76."

"Okay, then. Please help me sit him up."

Wilbur brushed us aside as he slowly heaved himself back to a sitting position, his legs remaining straight out on the extension at the foot of the exam table. Donna stepped to the side opposite me to raise the head of the table to about thirty degrees. Then she handed Wilbur a glass of water after waiting to see me nod that it was okay. "Now drink this and lie down please."

When he finished the water, I stood close to the table where I could grab him. Donna positioned herself on the other side.

He still looked a little dazed. "What do you reckon happened to me?"

"I'm not sure, but let's review some things. You said your shirt is new."

"That's right. My daughter bought it about a week ago."

"Were you wearing it the day of the accident?"

"Sure was. I think it looks right smart. I've worn it every day since."

"Your collar seems fairly tight. I want to check a couple of things."

"Have at it, Doc. I'm ready as I'll ever be."

After retrieving my stethoscope, I gently placed it over his right and then his left carotid arteries, listening to each one for several seconds. "I don't hear any bruits. That's good."

"You don't hear what?"

"Bruits. That means abnormal sounds when your heart pumps blood through them. If I had heard a bruit, that could mean a developing blockage in the artery. However, even without a bruit, you might still have some degree of obstruction."

He shook his head. "I'm sure glad you know what all that mumbo jumbo means. You're about to make my head spin thinkin' about it."

"Now one more thing. Donna, please stand close on his right side. Since the EKG is still hooked up, I'm going to turn it on first." I flipped the switch and watched as the paper began to roll, recording his cardiac activity. "Now I'm going to gently massage his carotid artery on the right side. Donna, watch the EKG, please."

I hadn't massaged the right carotid artery for more than four seconds when Donna yelled, "Stop!"

Wilbur started to reel about as I glanced down at the recording. Normal EKG complexes, but heart rate thirty-five and dropping. I pushed the lever to lower the head of the table, motioning my intention to Donna.

We each grabbed a shoulder and I said, "Okay. Down we go."

Wilbur didn't lose consciousness. He just complained of

feeling woozy.

"Wilbur, I want you to lie still while I call my friend, Dr. Alan Hill. He's a cardiologist I'd like for you to see right away."

"Why's that?"

"I believe you have a syndrome called hypersensitive carotid sinus. When there is pressure over the arteries of the neck, a reflex causes your heart to slow to a dangerously low rate. Then you black out. It's a normal reflex in most people. However, in your case, your heart is overly sensitive, and the heart rate drops way too far. If I'm right, any sudden turn of the neck while wearing a collar that's too tight, might make you faint. The problem is more common in older men."

Wilbur squinted up his eyes and glared at me. "You sayin' I'm old?"

"I didn't mean to call you old. I'm just trying to explain what may be wrong."

He gave way to raucous laughter. "Just testin' you out. If you said I'm old, you'd sure be right. Now you just go call your cardiologist so he can check out the bruits, or whatever you said I have. Then do me a favor. Tell Mr. ER Smarty Pants that he don't know so much. He should've checked me for bruits."

Within about thirty minutes, I had arranged for Wilbur's daughter and son-in-law to take him to see Dr. Hill that afternoon. It turned out that my diagnosis of hypersensitive carotid sinus was correct. In some patients, medication alleviates the problem, but in his case, a permanent pacemaker was required to prevent bradycardic blackouts. If attacks are prolonged, such episodes can be dangerous and lead to permanent heart or brain damage.

Fortunately, Wilbur Harding had no further problems, but he still refuses to fasten the button at the top of his collar. When in town, he enjoys spinning yarns while sitting at the soda fountain in Barry House's general store and pharmacy. And he never fails to remind his farmer buddies to wear a loose collar.

Chapter 26:

Emergency Blood Work

"Doc, you've got to help me." Christine closed the break room door, wheeled around with a determined look in her eyes, and tromped to the table where I was completing a chart. Stopping before me, she folded her arms. "I've had all I can take this morning."

I looked up, perplexed. Normally, Christine could handle about anything. "What's the trouble?"

"In the first place, Mr. Wheeler came in to complain about his bill. He said you charged him too much. His insurance paid everything but $2.50. He claims he doesn't owe it. He wants you to look at the statement."

I reached for his statement, laid the chart down, and sat back. "Really? What's his problem? He always complains no matter what he's charged. But $2.50 owed out of a hospital bill of $525.00?" I stood up and started to pace. "I visited him at least twice daily for several days while he was in the ICU recovering from congestive heart failure. I can't believe he's complaining about the small amount he still owes."

She shook her head. "Well, he is. He wouldn't leave the window so I could check in other patients until I brought the bill to you for consideration."

I thought of all the times I went to see him, morning, evening, and in between if he became unstable. "Well, tell him I said he owes $2.50."

Christine looked pleased. "Good. I was hoping you'd say that. Last time, you wrote off a $5.00 bill the insurance didn't pay for him. I knew that was a mistake."

I had to chuckle. Christine rarely was that outspoken with me. She had to be really upset.

"Anything else bothering you?"

She made a pitiful face. "You might say that. The phone has been ringing off the wall. People are lined up at the window three deep. And Christopher and Minnie Johnston are about to drive me batty. They called me three times before 9:30 a.m., then showed up at the window demanding to be worked in for an emergency this morning."

"Didn't you give them an appointment?"

"Yes. For tomorrow morning, but that wasn't good enough."

"What's the emergency?"

"I don't know. I only work here doing my best to triage patients, but they claimed that it was a secret that couldn't be shared with me. How do you like that for clarity?"

"Can't you get them to come back tomorrow morning? We're really booked today."

"You're telling me. But I can't get them to leave unless you brought a 45-caliber pistol to work this morning."

Christine looked so distressed, but the situation now struck me funny. I covered my mouth with my hand trying to look serious, but quickly lost control and began to laugh.

Wide-eyed, briefly startled at my laughter, she began to shake with mirth, finally laughing as well.

Donna entered the room just then and stopped in her tracks. "Did I miss something funny or what?"

Christine regained her composure, whirled around, and marched toward the door to the waiting room. "Tell you later. Right now I have a bill to present, a phone to place back on the hook, and some people to confront. They can either have a seat or leave. So there!"

Donna shrugged. "Did I say something wrong?"

"No. Christine's just having a rough day. Mr. Wheeler is at the window. You know how he can act. And it's really busy just now.

She'll be all right. She was just venting when it struck me funny. I couldn't help but laugh and she joined in. It's hilarious."

"I have your next three patients in rooms. They're ready for you. Meanwhile, I'll go see if I can help her catch up." She turned and smiled mischievously. "What I really want to do is find out what's so funny. I know Christine very well. As soon as we're caught up, she'll tell me everything. She loves keeping me up to date on all the office gossip."

***

Two hours went by as we busily saw patients, doing our best to address every need. Mr. Wheeler had paid his $2.50 bill while complaining loudly in the waiting room about greedy doctors, and the Johnstons still awaited a turn to be placed in a room as work-in patients.

When Donna finally had Christopher and Minnie ready to be seen, she exited the room with a big smile on her face.

They were next, so I said, "What's so funny this time?"

"You'll find out soon enough. They're just too cute."

Now what? I shrugged and entered the room. After shaking their hands, I took a seat opposite them. "How can I help you today?"

They exchanged nervous glances, then looked up at me. Both were overweight, to put it mildly. Just plain simple folks.

Christopher acted as spokesman as Minnie sat quietly, hands folded in her lap. "We need to have emergency blood tests done today."

I scratched the back of my neck. "What are you talking about?"

Minnie blushed as Christopher continued, "We got to say our vows tomorrow."

Now I was totally confused. "What vows are you talking about?"

He smiled, then looked down at the floor. I could barely hear as he said, "Our marriage vows, Doc."

This didn't make any sense. "But you're already married,

206

aren't you?"

"Oh yeah. Ten years tomorrow. So the blood tests have to be done today." He looked at Minnie. "Right, sweetie?"

She nodded vigorously.

"You two didn't get a divorce or something?"

Christopher looked me in the eye. "Course not. We are repeating our vows in church tomorrow."

How could this all be happening in my office today? What had I done wrong? I coughed and cleared my throat. "You don't need blood tests just to resay your vows. You're already married."

A very serious look came over Christopher's face while Minnie appeared on the verge of tears. An uncomfortable silence ensued before he found his voice. "You aren't refusing to do our blood tests, are you?"

Now what did I say? I fumbled for words. "No. Not that. Not really. You just don't need them to resay your wedding vows."

They stared at me in disbelief before Christopher blurted out, "You're wrong. My cousin was my best man at our first wedding. He has a high school diploma. Real smart man. Smartest in our whole family. He said it's got to be done again or it won't be legal. He's my best man again tomorrow. Minnie's sister is standing up with her, just like before."

"Christopher, did you ask your minister about this?"

"Yeah. I did. He said we didn't need to do that, but we're taking no chances. So are you going to do our blood work or not?"

"I don't quite know what to say."

"Well, if you don't know what to say, I do. If you don't take our blood, we'll just have to find us a new doctor." They sat glaring in my direction in a silence so profound I could almost hear my heart beating.

As he started to stand, I managed to squeak out, "Just a second. Let me look at your charts."

Christopher was on medication for blood pressure and it had been nearly a year since his last blood work was done. Minnie had always refused in the past and had no tests at all.

I hoped this would work. "There are some blood tests you both need to have. Just sit in here and I'll have Donna come and draw your blood."

Christopher relaxed and scooted back in his chair. They were all smiles now. Minnie spoke for the first time. "Will our tests be back in time for you to sign our papers tomorrow? The wedding is at 3:00 p.m. Just like our first one."

"You'll have papers to sign?"

Christopher nodded eagerly. "Reverend White said he'd give us a certificate, just like ten years ago."

I sighed. "If you have papers to sign tomorrow, I'll sure sign them for you."

He sprang up, grabbed my hand, and began pumping it up and down. "Thanks a million, Doc. I'm sure glad you're our doctor. I really didn't want to change. You were just spoofing, weren't you?"

"Maybe I was spoofing myself."

Christopher threw his head back and laughed uproariously, then gave me a bone-jarring slap on the back. "Thanks, old buddy. You're all right."

Minnie nodded her agreement, and they left arm in arm after their blood was drawn.

They were the last patients of the morning, so I followed them to the waiting room, then watched them exit and go to their car.

As I stood staring out the front window, muffled laughter came from the reception office window. I turned to look, and Christine and Donna were convulsing with mirth. As the Johnstons pulled out of the lot, they gave vent to peals of laughter.

Christine finally regained control enough to speak. "Doc, did they teach you anything like this in school. I mean, did you feel like you were in over your head?"

I nodded grimly. "Way over my head, ladies. Way over."

The afternoon was relatively uneventful, but sure enough, the next day, Christopher hurried in at 2:30 p.m. and thrust his paper through the window to Christine. She managed to keep a straight face and brought it to me for my signature. It was an embossed form stating that one Christopher Johnston and one Minnie Johnston had repeated their marriage vows on such-and-such a date.

Donna passed me in the hallway after Christopher left.

"What? No rice to toss? How disappointing."

And so ended another exciting episode in the life of a country doctor.

Chapter 27:

That Strange Fruity Smell

The hot, sultry dog days of early August had arrived. Puffy white cumulus clouds floated in the deep blue sky while cicadas buzzed in the trees behind my office, their music waxing and waning, and I felt the lassitude of the environment to the full.

I needed a break. Working sixty to eighty hours a week was wearing me down. If my hours had been regular, it would have helped, but when I chose to deliver babies, scheduled times of rest and sleep were an idyllic relic of my dimly remembered past. In our small Indiana county, solo practice was the norm for several years after I hung out my shingle. There were no obstetricians closer than thirty miles. In addition, I made rounds every day unless physically out of town on the all-too-rare vacation, meaning about three hundred fifty-five workdays per year.

But I had hope. I had scheduled ten days of vacation with my family beginning the week prior to Labor Day. But alas, first things first. I had two more weeks until I could experience a much-needed respite.

I sat in my lab/break room in the back of my office polishing off my second cup of black coffee while gazing out the back window. A large flock of blackbirds covered our neighbor's pasture, no doubt storing up energy for their anticipated long flight south in another month. I sighed. How I wished I could join them on their coming journey. Three sorrel horses kicked up dust, scattering the flock, as they moved up to graze near the fence line. What a pity. No rest, even for the hungry blackbirds.

My reverie came to an end as Christine barged into the room, slamming the door behind her. "Dr. Matlock, there's a very sick man in the waiting room. Donna's not here. She ran to the pharmacy to get a vial of penicillin from Barry House. Patients are just starting to arrive, and I'm not sure what to do with him. He looks like he's about to collapse."

I jumped up, nearly upsetting my cup. "Sure. Let's go."

A tremulous, diaphoretic elderly man of normal body habitus leaned against the wall beside the reception window, supported by Mark Harrison, one of my patients. "Doc, this is Jane's grandfather. He and his wife just arrived for a visit this morning. They drove in from central Ohio. I don't know how she got him to our house. Can we set him down somewhere?"

Christine grabbed a folding chair from the reception area and shoved it under him as he collapsed onto it, his gray hair tumbling over his forehead, sweat dripping down his face as he gasped rapidly for breath, slumping forward on the chair, barely conscious.

I knew we only had minutes to act. I motioned to Christine. "Get the wheelchair from the lab. We need to lay him down on an exam table." I knelt beside him, attempting a cursory exam as Christine ran for the wheelchair. Instantly noting the fruity odor of his breath, I asked, "Is he diabetic?"

Mark shook his head. "Not that I know of, but this is Wade Cramer, my wife's grandfather. Jane and her grandmother, Hettie Cramer, should be here any minute."

Donna entered the front door with Jane Harrison and an elderly woman I took to be Hettie Cramer as Christine arrived with the wheelchair. Mark and I bodily lifted Mr. Cramer into the wheelchair and hurriedly transported him to exam room 1, where we then lifted him onto the exam table.

Jane and her grandmother joined us in the room while Mark stepped out into the hall to make more room for Donna and me to work. Donna moistened a washcloth in the sink and placed it on Mr. Cramer's forehead. His eyes opened and he nodded his thanks.

Donna bent over beside the cart to check his vital signs while I turned to the family. "What can you tell me about Mr. Cramer?"

Jane seated her grandmother and answered, "Granddad is a traveling evangelist. He just closed out a meeting in Harrisburg, Pennsylvania, and was on his way to visit us. He didn't feel well, and they stayed overnight at a motel in Columbus, Ohio. Grandma Cramer had to drive the rest of the way today, but I think they should have stopped at a hospital before coming to our house."

Donna looked up. "Blood pressure 90/58. Pulse 110, respirations 28."

Mrs. Cramer brushed tears from her eyes with a tissue Jane handed her. "He was sick all day yesterday, but he wanted to get here as soon as possible. I wanted him to stop at a hospital along the way, but he's a stubborn man. I guess we made a mistake. Is he going to be all right?"

I glanced at Donna. "Call Art McKay and get him on the way." As an afterthought, I added, "And tell Christine to reschedule everybody for later this week." I turned my attention to Wade Cramer. "Reverend, can you hear me?"

He opened his eyes and was able to speak in a weak voice. "Yes. I feel a little better since I got my head down."

"Are you diabetic?"

He shook his head.

"Are you taking any medication?"

Again he responded by shaking his head.

I continued a brief examination, noting fruity breath accompanying his rapid breathing, and his dry mouth, sallow complexion, and clammy extremities. He appeared to be in impending shock from dehydration and metabolic acidosis.

Donna soon returned to assist me. Within minutes, she handed me his EKG, which showed some nonspecific changes along with a sinus tachycardia, a rapid but otherwise normal cardiac response to acute illness. There was no sign of heart attack.

Donna continued to monitor Reverend Cramer. "Blood pressure up to 98/60, pulse still 110. Fingerstick blood glucose greater than 600."

I pulled up a chair close to Mrs. Cramer. "Your husband has new-onset diabetes. Can you give me any more details while we wait for the ambulance? When did he first get sick?"

"He tried to hide it from me, but he's not been eating much and has been vomiting the last two days. I asked him what was wrong when he kept having me stop at gas stations along the way today. He admitted that he was stopping to vomit and to empty his bladder. And what is that strange fruity smell on his breath? Is that just from vomiting?"

"I'm afraid not. That fruity smell is due to ketones in the body and bloodstream. It's called diabetic ketoacidosis. Did you hear the nurse mention his blood glucose of over 600?"

"Yes, that sounds high, but I don't know what it means. You mentioned diabetes, but he's never been diabetic before."

"It means that he has developed acute-onset diabetes. That type is more common in children and young adults. The pancreas is the organ that makes insulin. It has apparently ceased to function quite suddenly. That fruity odor is due to ketones, or acetone, produced by the body because of the decompensation of his pancreas. His blood sugar is probably much higher than 600, but that's all the higher the small portable meter will go. I have no doubt that he is dehydrated. That's why his blood pressure is low, that and acidosis. He urgently needs IV fluids, and he's going to the hospital as soon as the ambulance gets here. If you'll excuse me, I'm going to call ahead for an ICU bed."

Within twenty minutes, Art McKay arrived with his chief EMT, Willie Robertson, and we had Reverend Cramer fastened on a cart and ready to go in the ambulance. I jumped in the back with Willie, hoping to prod Art into driving faster than his usual fifty miles per hour on the highway. I sat beside the head of the cart while Willie placed a blood pressure cuff on Reverend Cramer's left arm and began monitoring the vital signs.

Art flipped the switch turning the siren and lights on, then glanced back to see if we were ready. "All set, fellas?"

"All set, and let's hurry," I answered. "He needs IV fluids as soon as possible."

Art saluted me with his right index and long fingers. "Will do. Hang on." With that, he pulled out onto the road and accelerated to his usual emergency speed of fifty miles per hour, although the posted speed was fifty-five.

I cringed, groaning softly. "Can't we go a little faster?"

Art looked back. "What's that? You say I'm going too fast?"

"No, Art. It's okay with me if you go a lot faster."

"As soon as we get to the interstate, I'll pour it on."

Meanwhile, Art continued without any added acceleration for the approximately two miles to the interstate highway. As he merged with traffic once there and quickly moved to the passing lane, he called over his shoulder, "Okay, hang on, fellas. Here we go."

From where I sat, I could see the speedometer as it edged up to fifty-five in the seventy-mile-per-hour speed zone. As cars and trucks whizzed by us on the right side, I tried relaxing, knowing that further protest would be in vain.

Willie noticed my frustration and patted me on the shoulder. "It'll be okay, Doc. At least you got him over fifty miles per hour. Believe me, that's an accomplishment."

I looked down at Reverend Cramer and noticed him staring anxiously up at me. Not wanting him to be apprehensive, I simply said, "We'll soon have you in the hospital and feeling better."

It was at times like these that I wished we had IV fluids available in the office to start on the way to the hospital. Most of the rural ambulances still didn't have advanced EMTs who could start and administer IVs. At least he did have oxygen by nasal canula in the ambulance, but due to the acidosis, he continued to breathe rapidly as his body tried to overcome acidosis by hyperventilating.

***

Thirty minutes later, we arrived at the hospital. Willie and I hopped out of the ambulance, then pulled the cart out, pausing only briefly to raise it before continuing through the ER entrance's double doorway. Art joined us as we wheeled the cart toward the elevator to the second floor, where ICU was situated.

Linda Ottinger and Liz O'Conner rushed to assist as we

rolled the cart into the ICU. Once they had Reverend Cramer in bed, Linda performed a venipuncture with a large catheter, drew off blood for the lab, and attached an IV of normal saline running wide open for the first liter of fluid.

ICU was a beehive of activity as the radiology tech took a portable chest X-ray, a phlebotomist arrived to draw an arterial blood gas, and nursing assistants attached a cardiac monitor to the patient and assisted the nurses in caring for him.

Art McKay sat at a table near the nurses' station filling out his paperwork for the run. When he had finished, he approached to get my signature on the form. "Thanks for riding with us. I always feel better when you can come along."

"I was glad to. Reverend Cramer is very critical. I didn't know if we would get him here in time."

"When you finish here, I'll be glad to come back and take you home. You just say the word."

I smiled at Art. No one could stay upset at him for long. "That's very kind of you. I might take you up on that later if my wife is unable to come and get me."

Willie sauntered over and nudged Art in the ribs. "What Doc and I really want to know is why you drove all the way here in the passing lane on the interstate at fifty-five miles per hour?"

Art looked momentarily puzzled before answering. "Willie, I'd drive that fast any day of the week for Doc. Sure, it's dangerous, but it's all part of our job. It's what we signed up for."

As Art went to retrieve the ambulance cart, Willie grinned and shrugged before following him to the door. "What can you say to that, Doc? Art really thinks he drove here fast. He's one of a kind."

"That he is, Willie. One of a kind."

Linda handed me the results of the blood gases as Liz began implementation of the orders. "You had better look at this. His blood pressure is up to 100/70 but the pulse is still about 110 to 112 with continued Kussmaul respirations (rapid breathing associated with acidosis). His stat blood sugar is 950, but he is more alert and talking a little."

Arterial blood gas: pH 7.05, pO2 98, pCO2 25. (Normal values are pH 7.4, pO2 100, pCO2 40. These are approximations used in calculations of acid-base balance in individual patients. In addition, normal values vary from laboratory to laboratory.)

"Start regular insulin at 10 units IM hourly with serum electrolytes. Blood sugar, BUN, and creatinine every two hours. Run the first unit of saline in rapidly, then slow to 250 ml per hour until I can reassess him."[4]

Linda nodded and hurried away to start insulin as I quickly added the verbal orders on the order sheet to those already written.

Liz approached as I finished writing, then handed me the electrolytes. "Reverend Cramer's family is in the ICU waiting room."

"I'll be with them as soon as I examine him once more."

At the bedside, I noted that the sweating had abated and he was definitely more alert. He was still too ill to speak much, but the saline was having a beneficial effect as the monitor registered his latest blood pressure at 115/75 and pulse down to 106. His heart, lungs, and general examination were otherwise non-revealing. "How are you feeling? Any better?"

He nodded and mouthed, "Some better."

"Any pain?"

"Just a little abdominal pain, but not too much."

"You're looking better already. I'll be back in a little while. Let the nurses know if you need anything."

He nodded, and I proceeded to the waiting room to speak with his family.

Mark and Jane Harrison anxiously awaited with Hettie Cramer when I entered the room. Fortunately, no other families were present at the time.

I pulled up a chair opposite the family. "Reverend Cramer is conscious, more alert, and responding to the IV therapy already. His blood pressure is coming up and his pulse is slowing just a bit. He's very dehydrated from the acute onset of diabetes."

Hettie spoke up. "Thank goodness he's better, but I don't

---

[4] Regular insulin was just being popularized as an IM (intramuscular) dosage hourly for DKA in the 1970s. It worked very well then but hasn't been given IM for DKA for many years. No doubt physicians in training today would throw their hands up in horror at many of the treatments that were popular at that time in the history of medicine.

understand how he got sick so fast."

"There are two predominant types of diabetes, type 1 and type 2. Type 1 diabetes is more common in the young, but adults can get it as well. It occurs when the pancreas suddenly ceases making insulin, at least in any significant amount. Perhaps a virus caused it. But whatever the cause, we know that is what's wrong. Type 2 is considered adult onset, usually associated with obesity and is of a slow onset."

"How did he get so dehydrated?" Mark asked. "Hettie said he was still trying to drink water, even though he later admitted to vomiting in service-station restrooms."

"The kidneys cannot reabsorb that much sugar being released once insulin stops working. Basically, as sugar is eliminated in the urine, body water goes with it. That alone lowers blood pressure due to ongoing dehydration."

Linda joined us, handing me the most recent labs. "Reverend Cramer is awake enough to ask for Mrs. Cramer. He's worried that she will think he's 'seriously ill.' He wants to reassure her that he'll be just fine." She smiled and excused herself.

I perused the most-recent lab data. Serum sodium 132, potassium 5.5, serum bicarb 7. A UA was positive for bacteria and many white blood cells, indicating UTI.

"These labs are about what I expected, except he also has a urinary tract infection. His sodium is a little low but will normalize as he improves. The potassium is elevated, but in truth, there is a total body potassium deficit with acute diabetic ketoacidosis, and we will be carefully starting potassium very soon. His serum bicarb level is only 7. Normally, it is around 25 to 30 with a little variation. It simply means that he has an acid build-up in the body. That's why he's breathing fast. Hyperventilation in his case is totally involuntary. His body is trying to get rid of carbon dioxide, which is also an acid. As the metabolic acidosis caused by DKA subsides, he will slow his breathing automatically."

Jane asked, "Does Grandpa have a kidney infection?"

"Possibly, but it could be a prostate or bladder infection."

"He's had a history of prostate infections in the past," Hettie said.

"Whatever the exact cause, I'll be starting him on IV antibiotics. The infection may even be the problem that caused or at least contributed to the rapid deterioration of the pancreatic function."

Mark Harrison, a science teacher for junior high students, asked, "How about the digestive functions of the pancreas? Will they be affected as well?"

"Not usually. That would be very uncommon unless he has a history of chronic pancreatitis. You all told me he had been very healthy in the past, so I'm not worried about that."

Jane nodded. "That's right, he has been the picture of health. This is the first time I've even heard about prostate infections."

"He has been blessed with a robust constitution for most of his life," Hettie confirmed.

I stood up. "Any more questions before I go back to check on him?"

Hettie asked, "Can I see him soon? And will you be here while he is critical?"

"You should be able to see him in the near future, and yes, I plan to be here the rest of the day. This isn't a condition easily monitored except at the bedside."

She took my hand. "Thank you, Doctor, and God bless you."

***

That was a long but rewarding day as I did my hospital rounds, saw a few patients in the ER, and spent most of my time in the ICU monitoring lab reports and the patient's response to therapy. I was pleasantly surprised to see Art McKay coming through the doors of ICU at 9:00 p.m. that evening.

"Hello, Doc. How is our patient doing?"

"He's doing very well. Thanks for your help this morning."

Art grinned from ear to ear. "There's nothing more rewarding than helping people, is there?"

"You're right about that. By the way, can I still have that ride back home?"

"That's why I'm here. Just to offer you that ride."

***

Reverend Cramer recovered rapidly over the next few days and was eventually stabilized on a regimen of long-acting insulin and a diabetic diet as the short-acting regular insulin was gradually discontinued. His UTI, which turned out to be acute prostatitis, resolved nicely, and he was referred back to his family doctor on discharge from the hospital.

Chapter 28:

A Doctor Should Know Better

My longed-for rest had arrived at last. I was taking twelve days off at the end of August extending into September, returning to work after Labor Day. Dr. Langley had agreed to cover for me, including obstetric coverage while I was away. Life just couldn't get any better, or so I thought.

Although my three children were small, they enthusiastically took part in planning the family vacation. Cindy loved horses and cowboys, so I reasoned that a trip out West would be a wonderful idea. The only one with reservations was my wife, Janet. She preferred a short trip with a longer stay at a cabin in Gatlinburg. But we had already done that once, and I reasoned that Cindy, David, and Diane would be wonderful travelers now that Cindy was three years and ten months old, and the twins were eighteen months old. What could possibly go wrong?

My last workday was hectic, between tying up all the loose ends, making sure the OB patients had Dr. Langley's number, ensuring the last of the routine prescriptions were called in, and taking care of the innumerable little things that have to be done daily. I still arrived home at 7:00 p.m. Not a bad start.

Excitement was in the air as we had our evening meal. The children could hardly eat for talking about seeing cowboys, horses, and maybe a bear or two.

Next came packing. For the children, what dolls to take for Cindy and Diane, which stuffed animal for David, and so it went. Quieting them down for bedtime turned out to be much more difficult than I had anticipated, but by midnight they were finally tucked in and apparently sleeping soundly, at least I hoped so.

My head hit the pillow shortly after midnight, and I went to sleep at once. Fatigue had stalked my pathway until I fell asleep whenever I sat down in a comfortable chair at home, let alone when my head hit a pillow in a soft bed. My alarm was set for 7:00 a.m. Planned departure was scheduled for 8:30 a.m., give or take a little depending on the needs of three energetic little children.

At 3:30 a.m. my carefully worked-out plans began to fall apart when the phone rang.

I had become expert at finding a telephone with the lights out, so I quickly picked up the receiver hoping that the family still slept peacefully. I answered from force of habit. "Hello, this is Dr. Matlock."

"Doctor, this is Mildred on OB. We have your patient Evelyn Dillman. She's in active labor, dilated to seven centimeters, and this is her third pregnancy. You'd better get here right away."

"How long has she been there?"

"About twenty minutes now. I think she'll have this baby fairly quick."

"Mildred, don't you have my notice about Dr. Langley covering for my OB patients while I'm on vacation?"

"There's a note stating that as of 7:00 a.m., he will take call for you."

"Did you try to call him?"

"No, I didn't. Mrs. Dillman insists that she wants you to deliver the baby. She doesn't know Dr. Langley and doesn't wish him called."

I hoped she didn't hear my groan. "Okay. Tell her I'll be there."

"Thank you, Doctor."

My wife stirred as she heard me up dressing in the dark. "Carl, is it time to get up already?"

"No, dear."

"Then why are you up getting dressed? Can't you sleep?"

"No, I can't sleep. There's a patient in active labor, and I have to go right now."

She yawned sleepily, rolled over, and checked the luminous hands on the clock. "Oh, good. I have time to sleep a while yet."

I raced down the hall, stubbed my big toe in the dark, hopped about on one foot suppressing a yell, and finally found my way to the living room with my shoes and socks in hand to complete dressing.

Finally, I tore out the kitchen door, jumped in the car, remembered to raise the garage door at the last minute, then sped to the hospital hoping to meet no patrol cars. They wouldn't ticket me for an emergency, but I didn't have time for any stops if Mildred Long was correct in her assessment, and she usually was.

At the hospital, I fumbled with my key, finally got the side door open, then ran up the stairs to OB labor and delivery on the third floor. Mildred Long and Sharon Cunningham, the nursing assistant, were wheeling Evelyn Dillman to the delivery room on her cart, moaning and pushing, clutching the rails with both hands to increase her leverage.

Mildred smiled. "I think you have time to change if you're quick."

I nodded, ran into the doctors' dressing room, peeled off my clothes, threw on scrubs, and raced into the delivery room with just enough time to put on gloves as the baby's head of thick black hair was crowning. Evelyn pushed forcefully as I guided the delivery and thankfully avoided any perineal lacerations.

The baby began squalling as I suctioned out her nose and throat, announcing to the world her displeasure with this audacious doctor pestering her so soon after leaving the dark, warm comfort of the womb in exchange for the bright lights, cool air, and noise of the delivery room.

I sighed, feeling sorry for this little bundle of innocence. Poor baby. It's a cruel world. I thought of my warm bed and lost sleep. I could identify with the displeasure of this newborn.

Ninety minutes later, I had checked little Miss Dillman, weighing in at six pounds and seven ounces, and found her to be quite healthy. I had also finished dictating a delivery note and written a brief summary in the chart for Dr. Langley. It would be a while before the dictated note was transcribed. Finally, I checked with Mrs. Dillman.

She smiled and said, "Thanks. I'm glad you took care of me. Have a great time on your vacation. You deserve it."

Feeling a little guilty, I grinned. "Thanks. I'll see you for a post-partum exam in four weeks."

I stopped by the cafeteria for a cup of coffee, hoping it would help me wake up. The cooks always had a pot going for the doctors and any overnight visitors. Glancing at the wall clock, I saw that it was already 5:45 a.m. By the time I got home it would be after 6:00 a.m., with less than an hour to sleep. So I sat down in the cafeteria and had not one but three cups of coffee before going home to shave, wash up, and prepare to depart for my time of rest.

Arriving home, I found that Janet already had the kids up, dressed, and ready to go. We ate a quick breakfast of cereal and milk, and she gave their faces a once over with a washcloth for the last time before departure.

I had a Chevrolet Caprice at that time, a spacious car by today's standards, which with three small children on a journey of thousands of miles is a good thing. I took a country road to the interstate approximately ten miles from home.

The children were sound asleep in the back seat before we got five miles down the road, but my first indication of trouble occurred as I merged onto the interstate. Cindy awakened and said, "Are we 'bout there yet? Are we to da motel?"

Janet turned around. "No, sweetheart. Go back to sleep."

Fortunately, she drifted right back to sleep, but it was an omen of things to come. I, for one, began fighting sleep after only a couple of hours of driving time. I began making frequent rest stops, finally pulling into a rest area to sleep for a few minutes.

An hour later found me back on the highway, hypnotized by a white line down the middle of the road that seemed to be wobbling from side to side. I knew then that we would not be able to make the first day's destination. I looked over at my wife. "We're going to have to stop early. I can't drive too much farther."

My wife, a very pleasant and agreeable person, merely

answered, "Whatever you think, dear."

The next day found us on our way to West Yellowstone, Montana, by way of the Black Hills of South Dakota, Mount Rushmore, and Yellowstone National Park. I had a lot more to learn about the West than I realized. Distances on a map are deceivingly finite while driving time with small restless children quickly becomes infinite, or so it seems.

David and Diane loved one another very much. They still do today, but putting them in the back seat of a car at such a tender age with inadequate resources to keep them occupied was asking for trouble. Sibling affection has definite limits, as any knowledgeable parent can testify. Janet spent a lot of the trip settling arguments and refereeing who got what toy and when. Cindy did better, but she tired quickly with the long riding times between motels.

We followed secondary highways in order to really see the country, sometimes passing signs with such warnings as *Last service station for 125 miles* or—even better—*Open range, watch for cattle.* Those warnings kept me busy watching the gasoline gauge and the road for possible bovine obstructions.

I also soon received an education on Western restaurants. Stopping for breakfast in South Dakota, we ordered a breakfast plate for each child as well as for ourselves. I noticed the waitress smiling a lot as we ordered for the children, but I thought she was just being friendly. My heart skipped a few beats and my wife gasped as they were each served a plate with mountains of pancakes floating in maple syrup, multiple slices of bacon, and three scrambled eggs. She didn't bring the coffee, but they had a huge pitcher of milk to share. No wonder it was called the Cowboy Special. The kids loved it, but we learned that they could easily share a "Western plate" among all three and still have leftovers.

We enjoyed our stay of three nights in West Yellowstone at a motel with all cowboy décor. Even the overhead lights were mounted on a large wagon wheel. We also had plenty of time to drive through Yellowstone National Park and were lucky enough to see some buffalo and a moose or two.

I was just beginning to feel rested, but then I made my fatal mistake. I sat on the bed the last night in the West Yellowstone motel studying the map. It all looked so doable. My wife was getting the children in their pajamas for the night, when I made a strategic mistake, one sure to test my wife's love and devotion for me (and did I say, she's a patient lady). "I have an idea, dear."

Recognizing the sheepish look on my face, she answered slowly, "What's that?"

"I was just studying the atlas. I've never been to Pike's Peak before. I'd love to drive up the mountain and see the West from a different vista."

She didn't even take time to think that one through. "It's too far. Not a good idea."

I don't remember all my finely tuned arguments regarding the advantage of viewing more of the West—in particular, Pike's Peak in Colorado—but somehow Janet reluctantly consented, probably because she was too tired to debate the issue as I recited the many glorious facts. "Pike's Peak is over fourteen thousand feet in elevation, named by the American explorer, Zebulon Pike. Isn't that something?"

I suddenly realized that I was getting no response after several minutes extolling the virtues of the mountain as a great tourist spot to visit. Glancing over, I realized that she had gone to sleep, but she had consented. I was very happy as I got ready for bed, still planning all the things we would do the next day.

The trip to Pike's Peak from West Yellowstone was my undoing. As I said, distances are deceiving in the West. Everything is supersized, especially the highways that go on forever and ever. The kids were increasingly fussy in the backseat, and Janet had little to say. She seemed to be losing interest in our trip. Ouch. A bad sign.

It was with relief that I pulled into our motel in Colorado Springs, Colorado, at 3:00 a.m. It was with chagrin that I learned the checkout time was an unreasonable 9:00 a.m. I tried to make a funny remark to make Janet laugh. "Well, we'll just have to sleep fast."

When all I got was a shrug of her shoulders, I decided to forgo levity and hurriedly unloaded the car. We turned in as soon as possible, but morning indeed came all too soon. We definitely hadn't slept "fast enough."

I noticed that for some reason, except for the kids chattering a little, breakfast was an otherwise quiet affair. I wisely decided to study the morning newspaper while my family finished eating and prepared to depart for our trip up Pike's Peak.

I tried extolling the beauty of the mountain and the far away vistas as we slowly labored up the mountain in our blue Caprice. The engine labored some, and it only got a little hot, but not enough to boil as some other unfortunate travelers were experiencing. And then we reached the summit. On stepping from the vehicle, I felt like my feet and legs were made of jelly. In fact, my whole body felt tremulous. I shook my head. Must be the altitude.

Next, I noticed all the people lined up breathing from oxygen masks at the welcome center near the crest of the mountain. I turned to mention it to Janet. "Dear, I didn't know they had emergency oxygen at the summit."

With alarm, I noticed that her face and lips were mildly cyanotic. She was also very tremulous. She has asthma and wasn't tolerating the rapid change in elevation accompanied by the lowered oxygen level in the atmosphere at the top of Pike's Peak.

All she could say was, "Carl, we have to go back down. Now!"

I never doubted for a moment that it was necessary. She would not be the first or the last to develop problems at such extreme elevations. Being unacclimated, neither of us were really able to appreciate the "beautiful vistas" I had fantasized about the day before.

Thankfully, the children seemed to tolerate the trip to the top much better than either one of us. We made it down in record time considering the winding highway we had to traverse. While resting at a more reasonable elevation at a highway rest stop several minutes later, I promised myself not to make any more unnecessary detours.

Janet's brief glance in my direction aroused intense guilt feelings in me that morning as we sat in a restaurant, slowly recovering from our experience. She finally found her voice after taking another puff from her asthma inhaler. "Can we please go home now."

Quite chastened now, I nodded, reached across the table for her hand, and simply said, "Yes, good idea."

I wish I could say that was the last of the adventure, but we were near Colorado Springs, miles from our home in Indiana. To top it all off, it was the Saturday of Labor Day Weekend. Never one to be daunted, I was certain I could find a motel vacancy somewhere along the way home.

I began driving, and driving, and driving. Interstate I-70 to Indianapolis is a long, long road. By the time I thought about a motel, it was about 3:00 p.m. and *No Vacancy* signs were out everywhere I looked. No problem. I decided to drive to a bigger city. There had to be something somewhere, didn't there?

Later in the afternoon, I realized that we were entering Abilene, Kansas, where the boyhood home of Dwight Eisenhower and the Eisenhower Presidential Library and Museum were located. I then proceeded to announce my next great idea. "Let's stop at the Eisenhower Center. I visited here with my family as a young boy. We can get a break from the road and maybe find a motel nearby afterward."

I pulled into the gigantic parking lot of the Eisenhower Center, locked the car, and guided my family to the entrance, where we were met by the doorkeeper. I pulled out my wallet to pay the entrance fee but was stopped by the kind gentleman. "I'm sorry, sir, but the museum closes in fifteen minutes. You'll have to come back tomorrow."

Somewhat downcast, I shepherded my family back to the parking lot, reached into my pocket for the key, and discovered to my mortification that it was locked in the car. I could see it in the ignition as I gazed helplessly through the side window. Unfortunately, Janet's extra key had been inadvertently left at home.

Panic stricken now, I gazed wildly about for a coat hanger, a wire, anything I could bend and force down beside the window to open the latch. Alas, there is a relative paucity of such items in the parking lot of a museum.

Looking sorrowfully about, I looked back at my longsuffering companion. "Sorry, dear. There's a service station about a half mile down the road. I'll walk there and see if I can get someone to come open the door."

Not surprisingly, she had little to say.

That was a day when telephone calls had to be made at phone booths after depositing the appropriate coins, and no booths were to be seen, so I began trudging my weary way to the gas station, hoping I would find help there. I hadn't noticed how hot it was until then, but I finally arrived at the station, mopping sweat from my brow with my handkerchief.

A friendly young man was on duty alone at the station. I introduced myself and relayed my plight. "Can you help me get back in my car?"

"Sure thing, Mister. But it'll be about an hour. I'm the only one working and I have to close up at 6:00 p.m. before I can come and help you."

At least it was a start. I thanked him profusely and retraced my steps back to the Eisenhower Center parking lot. When I arrived back at the car, the children were fussing about being hungry and my wife simply nodded when I relayed the message. Somehow my restful vacation was coming unglued.

At 6:15 p.m., my fears that the young man had forgotten us were allayed. He pulled up in the service-station wrecker, hopped out with a handy gadget to open car doors, and had us back inside within another minute. "Sorry you had to wait."

"That's okay. We're just happy to see you now. What do I owe you?"

"You had to wait quite a while, and I'm on my way home anyway. Just count it as a favor." He hopped back in the truck and sped off before I could hand him the tip I was fishing for in my wallet.

I only wish that had been the end of our tribulations, but after a restful meal at a nice restaurant, we found every motel taken along the way. No exceptions in spite of multiple stops for inquiry. At the last place in Saint Louis, the motel owner called around checking for me, but finally said, "I'm sorry, sir, but there are just no beds anywhere close. Labor Day Weekend, you know."

"I know. Thanks for trying."

I returned to the car, where Janet received the news stoically. "Well, can you drive on in?"

"I'm sure going to try. We may have to stop and sleep in the car at a rest area for a while, but we'll get home sometime."

Thankfully my family all slept as the sky darkened, and I finished the long drive home across Illinois, then on to our Indiana home, just about one thousand miles with no rest and irritable, exhausted children in the backseat.

We arrived home as day was dawning on Sunday morning. Janet had little to say at the time, but she really didn't need to say anything. My forlorn expression said it all. We spent the day catching up on sleep and rested all the next day, forgoing any further Labor Day celebrations.

I never thought it would come to this, but I finally had to admit, I needed to go back to work on Tuesday to rest. My vacation wore me and my entire family out. One would think that a doctor should know better.

A lot of years have come and gone since that time. Janet and I recently celebrated our forty-ninth wedding anniversary. She would still tell you that I like long drives, just not that long. It was anything but funny then, but it is hilariously entertaining to reminisce about now. During family gatherings on the holidays, we enjoy a good laugh about that "restful" vacation, including our less than ten minutes of glory at the summit of Pike's Peak.

Dear Reader,

Thanks for reading *Reminiscence: Life of A Country Doctor.* I hope you enjoyed the experience. If you would like to keep informed of my future releases and newsletters, please visit my webpage to subscribe at https://www.carlmatlockmd.com.

I can also be reached via my Facebook page: Carl Matlock, MD / Author.

My other books include the following:

1. *Rebel Against the Eagle,* paperback edition with study guide and a newer e-book edition of the same book without the study guide entitled *Rebels, Romans, and the Rabbi: A Story of Jewish Romance, Rebellion, and Reconciliation.*

2. *Jerusalem Crucible.*

3. *The Annals of A Country Doctor.*

Reviews on Amazon.com are appreciated.

A sample of my book, Jerusalem Crucible, is included beginning on the next page for your preview.

Thanks again,

Carl Matlock, MD

Spring 33 AD

Pontius Pilate gazed absentmindedly at the spume atop the whitecaps riding the deep-blue waves lashing the shore of Caesarea Maritima, the unrelenting restlessness of the Mediterranean reflecting the turbulence within him. He drew his toga tighter, shivering a little as the wind gusts battered him, chilling the depths of his soul. Low dark clouds scudded toward him in threatening ranks as distant lightning flared, the rumble of thunder shaking the shifting sands beneath his feet.

The last few years in this forsaken land had left him with a bitterness of heart that even the glowing smile of Claudia, his beloved wife, could not quench. Bitter bile rose even now, burning his throat, as his hair, sparse though it might be, blew in total disarray before the onslaught of the threatening tempest.

His personal guard, under the command of the faithful Centurion Lucius, stood at a seemly distance, watching him clench and unclench his right fist while holding his toga close about his body with his left. Knowing his moods too well, they waited for him to speak, not daring to break his muse.

In the way of Roman soldiers, they would protect him to the end. Lucius would send the entire squad to its death without a second thought if Pilate appeared endangered. The guard would respond, to the last man, without regard for personal safety. He was their lifeline to Rome, the city they loved and revered. More than that, each one had been in his service during the occupation of this troubled land. Nevertheless, they had more than a little fear and awe of this man with the volcanic personality.

Pilate had appropriated the palace built by Herod the Great on the famous harbor, also constructed under the direction of the evil genius of the unloved king. Pilate appreciated the comforts built into the fortress, never ceasing to marvel at the engineering feats accomplished at Caesarea. His only real solace, besides the nearness of his wife, was this stately residence by the sea.

He pivoted to his right and paced while large drops of rain stung his face as the gale grew in fury. His only thoughts centered on the argument he had just had with Claudia. As usual, he had lost. Why couldn't he just tell her no? He commanded life and death of every living being in Palestine—everyone, that was, except the bewitching woman whom he proudly called his wife.

Pilate truly wanted to please her. But when she had announced she would accompany him to Jerusalem for the Passover festival, he had shouted at her in dismay. Didn't she know it was dangerous? Hadn't she heard of the Zealots lying in wait to kill and maim Roman soldiers? In response, she had just smiled sweetly at him. He had thrown his hands up and left the palace for this seaside walk, trying to quiet his anger and still his anxious fear.

He hated this loathsome place, this land of the most rebellious subjects of Rome. They refused to worship the gods that he served, atheists in his eyes. Even worse, Emperor Tiberius had granted them special privileges of worship, in order to maintain the peace, and of course to keep the rich bribes coming from the wealthy Sadducees.

Tiberius. That name always caused him to grimace a little. At least the storm would mask his fear from the guard. Once again, he rehearsed the speech Tiberius had given him last: Pilate was to keep the peace and pander to the Jews.

How would he keep the peace in the seething cauldron of Jerusalem, protect his naïve wife, and avoid a violent clash with the rebels? Bah! The assignment was impossible. His own priorities were to placate Tiberius and please Claudia, but not necessarily in that order. He must indulge the Jews, but he hated them for it. The elite of the priestly caste, the Sadducees, especially assumed such airs appropriate only for despots.

Glancing up, he eyed his guard. They stood in silence, misery in their eyes as rain and wind buffeted them. With a twinge of guilt, he motioned to Lucius and his second-in-command to lead on. Others brought up the rear in their procession back to the shelter of the palace.

Night closed in early as the sun faded in the blackness of the gathering storm, sinking into the tossing billows of the Mediterranean. In the palace awaited a sumptuous evening feast near a roaring fire built for his comfort in the great blackened fireplace. He would smile at Claudia as if nothing unusual had happened and drink himself senseless once more. The pain of serving in this land and the responsibility of keeping the peace weighed like a boulder on him.

Tomorrow he must begin preparations for the annual journey to Jerusalem, but he didn't look forward to the Passover feast.

Jerusalem Crucible: Available on Kindle Unlimited
and as
Paperback Edition.

Made in the USA
Monee, IL
19 October 2021

80221877R00142